Here's to harnessing the
power of liminal space.
Onward,

"Rick Simmons is one of the most innovative and impactful leaders in the world. He leads with personal excellence and unparalleled emotional agility. *Unleashed* is an unprecedented resource on the power of liminal space—the gap between 'what was' and 'what's next'—and how to maximize pivotal transitions. This book captures the transformational magic of liminal space and how you utilize it in every area of life to become your best self."

—**Alan Stein,** *Keynote Speaker and Author*

"Compelling and incisive argument for harnessing the hidden power of liminality and discontinuity."

—**Joseph Glick,** *Senior Director, Deutsche Bank*

"Rick and the telos team helped me navigate the C-suite but more importantly guided me through a life-changing and unexpected brush with mortality. I came away from the life- and career-altering experience feeling better about myself and my place. Count me as a believer in the teachings of Rick, Amy, and the telos family."

—**Julian Kim,** *MD, Physician, Executive, Surgeon, and Educator*

"When Rick first shared the concept of liminal space with us I'm not sure I fully appreciated it. Looking back now at times when our business has been in liminal space Rick has always been my first phone call for advice. Learning how to harness this we now seek it out as an opportunity for growth and change."

—**Kelcey Lehrich,** *CEO, 365 Holdings*

"Inflection points, or liminal periods, big and small occur on a near continual basis—whether you recognize them or not. This book will help you harness and make the most of the change induced by external pressures, and it will also help you create ones to bring your organization, your team, or yourself further toward your goals."

—**Douglas Rhee,** *MD, Chair, University Hospitals Eye Institute and Case Western Reserve University School of Medicine*

"As friend and executive coach, Rick helped me celebrate the past while guiding my thinking for the future, on both a personal and professional level, as I wound down a rewarding work career. Recently retired, I look forward to putting to practice the concepts outlined in *Unleashed: Harnessing the Power of Liminal Space*, a new book by Rick and Amy Simmons, cofounders of the telos institute, as I proceed along the continuum of my own life's journey."

—**Mark R. Belgya,** *Fortune 500 CFO (retired) and Independent Director*

"Having participated in a telos leadership venture experience with my son in Israel, I have seen firsthand the power of curated liminality. There is no better process to reconnect, reexamine, and reimagine your direction. We have experienced our paths and lives in a very new and fulfilling way."

—**A. Mark Zeffiro,** *Former Public Company CEO/CFO*

"Rick Simmons and Amy Simmons are catapulting our collective awareness forward. *Unleashed* is a masterfully crafted portal into helping us all recognize and leverage the transformative power of discontinuity at a time when it's more available and more crucial than ever. Well done!"

—**Michael Anderson,** *MD, Senior Advisor to the US Department of Health and Human Services*

"Every person will move into liminal spaces through their personal and business lives. The telos institute gives these people the ability to identify these times and a vast set of tools to excel through and become better people and leaders, potentially accomplishing significantly more than they ever thought possible."

—**Al Weiss,** *President of Worldwide Operations, Walt Disney Parks and Resorts (retired)*

"Rick Simmons and Amy Simmons shine an illuminating light on how to recognize and harness the transformative potential of discontinuity. If you are seeking an inflection in your business, relationships, or life, or just feel something is out of alignment, this book is a must-read!"

—**Geoff Tanner,** *Chief Marketing and Commercial Officer, The J.M. Smucker Co.*

"*Unleashed* will help you unlock the power of purpose. It is a rich blend of wisdom, compassion, and practice that will help you turn breakdowns into breakthroughs."

—**Richard Leider,** *Best-Selling Author of* The Power of Purpose *and* Repacking Your Bags

"So great of the telos founders to share their special insights into how embracing uncertainty and ambiguity can drive personal growth and organizational development."

—**Neal J. Meropol,** *MD, Vice President, Head of Medical and Scientific Affairs, Flatiron Health*

"Whether we like it or not we are all at an inflection point, dealing with physical risks and emotional stress, economic challenges, and the country's political divide. Who isn't at least a little uncomfortable and dealing with change, whether it be health safety protocols, reengineering your business or career, or figuring out how to stay connected with family and friends? *Unleashed*, artfully written by Rick and Amy Simmons, shares their thought provoking experiences and their timing couldn't be better. Congrats to you both."

—**Dave Michelson,** *Board Member, Advisor, and Retired Public Company CEO*

"Rick and Amy have used their collective expertise to help capitalize on our 'when,' not our 'why,' to help us evolve—in our business and personal lives—into better, more intelligent versions of ourselves. Knowing when to recognize, leverage, and learn from these periods of 'liminal space' has helped me become a better business owner, manager, overall person. The 'when' is now."

—**Dave Blosser,** *Owner, H&H Polishing; Managing Partner, Shipwatch Business Advisors*

"As our company approached significant organizational and leadership change, I found this book incredibly valuable and empowering. It enabled an awareness of the inflection point, or liminality, that allowed our leaders to grow … and ultimately thrive! An excellent learning experience for business and life!"

—**Tony Mercurio,** *President and Chief Executive Officer, National Interstate Insurance Corporation*

"The key to driving transformational change is knowing both how and when to do it. *Unleashed* provides the insights and tools to do both. We have trusted Rick and Amy Simmons to teach our key leaders these concepts."

—**Mark Smucker,** *CEO, The J.M. Smucker Co.*

"A dynamic duo! Rick and Amy have teamed together to provide a blueprint for navigating change and disruption. Their unique voice and perspectives quickly become evident through the stories and concepts shared in *Unleashed*. The principles described within apply to one's professional and personal life and enable one to convert ambiguity and crisis into opportunities for growth, success, and contentment. In fact, their framework will not only lead to one's acceptance of disruption but an innate desire to create it! *Unleashed* will cause you to look inward, to thoughtfully examine who you are, and to develop a plan to become the best version of yourself, just as Rick and Amy have done. I'm honored to know Rick and Amy, and I am forever grateful for the manner in which they've enabled me to recognize liminal space, embrace it with conviction, and come out of it a more resilient and purposeful leader."

—**Mike Toth,** *President, Westfield Bank*

"This is a bold book! Rick and Amy address something we have all experienced but rarely have the language to talk about with others, let alone fully understand ourselves. They give us that language and invite us on an important, reflective journey, with the two of them as our guides. *Unleashed* is a must-read for those who want to make purposeful advances in their self-awareness, their relationships, and in their careers. Rick and Amy help you make those advances by helping you discover the spaces that can become catalysts. This book opened my eyes to greater self-discovery."

—**Scott N. Taylor,** *PhD, Arthur M. Blank Endowed Chair for Values-Based Leadership and Associate Professor of Organizational Behavior, Babson College*

"Like skilled sherpas on the slopes of Mt. Everest, Rick and Amy adeptly guide us through their concept that disruption (treacherous terrain) and adversity (thin air) are not simply inevitable challenges to be endured but rather inspiring opportunities to be embraced in our life's journey. In this remarkable work, the authors reveal the importance of creating time, space, and place (liminality) for appropriate reflection to allow for the emergence of new possibilities as a result of adversity. This experiential approach brings us to a threshold where catalytic power and transformational growth in all domains of our being can flourish. Once experienced we are able to act with new clarity to confidently push forward or pivot with profound purpose and impact in our ascent to the summit. They further posit that we may even curate this strategy in the absence of true adversity to generate creative energy for positive change."

—**Edward M. Barksdale, Jr.,** *MD, Professor of Surgery and Pediatric Surgeon*

"Once again, Rick and Amy of the telos institute offer us the opportunity to discover professional, personal, and organizational growth through learning how to identify, create, and navigate liminal space. They help to make the complex more simple and guide us toward a path for taking advantage of the opportunities that liminal space gifts to each of us."

—**Joline Vernon Manning,** *CHRO, Tarkett North America*

"The deep experience partnering with Rick, Amy and the telos team have been amongst the most impactful in my personal and professional life. From camping under the stars in the Grand Canyon finding the purpose of my work on a telos leadership venture to discovering how to continue to rebalance the portfolio of my life around what matters most has been an amazing adventure. The perspective has helped me successfully navigate rapidly growing our own firm, evolving as a leader, serving as a better husband, and teaching our children important values. Thank you for being with me through the change and important inflection points on my journey."

—**Matt Pullar,** *Partner, Sequoia Financial Group*

"*Unleashed: Harnessing the Power of Liminal Space* provides a framework that is both practical and relatable. Taking the time to reflect on inflection points in life helped me better appreciate and harness the power of liminal space. I've been there and didn't know it… I'm there now and know it! That's where the power of opportunities exist! Enjoy the ride!"

—**John W. Arena,** *SVP and US Chief Commercial Officer, Lundbeck*

"As leaders, we often feel called to dispel the uncertainty, the ambiguity that arises in our businesses or teams as quickly as possible. This book is a brilliant wake-up call to the inspiration that can emerge by seeing, articulating, and then reflecting amidst disruption. But instead of leaving you floundering in the messiness of change, this book also provides a practical roadmap for taking concrete action and capturing the true power and full benefit of transformation. A must-read today more than ever."

—**Amy Held,** *Chief Strategy and International Officer, The J.M. Smucker Co.*

"A timely and relevant gem! Today, unlike any previous time in history, our world is experiencing disruption at warp speed. This book is extremely timely and relevant, revealing the dichotomy between uncertainty, disruption, or chaos and the rich opportunity that can be uncovered if liminal space is recognized and embraced for the future possibilities that lie within. Success in the dynamic and highly complex healthcare industry is dependent on resiliency during periods of chaos, disruption, and instability. *Unleashed* provides practical guidance to serve healthcare leaders or anyone who needs a roadmap to steer out of adversity to a destination of sustained transformation! A must-read in these challenging times!"

—**Teri Shoulder,** *RN, Chief Quality Officer, Alternate Solutions Health Network*

"This book gives hope. The reader will discover the process to transform the angst of instability into opportunities for growth. This is the perfect book to share with my team. A must-read annually.

—**Francoise Adan,** *MD, ABIHM, Director, UH Connor Integrative Health Network*

"Rick Simmons and the telos team have been incredible partners. They helped guide and shape our leadership team. Now we work together as a whole, genuinely appreciating, empowering, and utilizing each team member's strength. Working with telos has enabled us to fulfill our mission to improve others' lives through mental health and addiction services."

—**Vicki Clark,** *LPCC-S, President and CEO, Ravenwood Health*

"Rick and Amy Simmons are the antithesis of plug-and-play, rinse and repeat, presumptuous consultants that rush to common, almost categorized solutions. Instead, they help executives and organizations slow down, simplify, and own periods of inflection, discomfort, and disruption by introducing them to the true power and potential in embracing liminal moments along the journey."

—**Randall S. Myeroff,** *CPA, CGMA, Chief Executive Officer, Cohen & Company*

"A timely, transparent, and practical exploration into using liminal space to create change. If you have been waiting to do something differently, this book may help you realize that the time is now."

—**Bauback Yeganeh,** *PhD, President, Everidian*

"When I first saw 'liminal' in the title of this book my first instinct was … well, to grab a dictionary. Which I did. When I learned a bit more about this liminality and then fully immersed myself in *Unleashed* it all made such perfect sense. Rick and Amy Simmons have taken a complex notion and put it into a powerful and easily metabolized vocabulary. One which helps us identify the key inflection points in our careers and, more importantly, our lives. These moments are not something to 'get through' but rather opportunities. This book positions us to identify and understand these moments as they are happening rather than reflect on them when it's too late. You will in fact feel 'unleashed' once you have fully understood and embraced the concept of liminal space."

—**Bob Garry,** *Senior Vice President, Strategic Talent Management, Hackensack Meridian Health*

"Rick and the entire telos staff have been instrumental in helping me personally and our practice get aligned using our core values as our true north. This was especially helpful during the pandemic. I have enjoyed working with their staff in various projects and I can say we are a better group because of their insight into emotional intelligence and approach to leading high functional teams. To Rick, Amy, and telos, Bravo Zulu!

—**Jorge Garcia-Zuazaga,** *MD, Founder and President, Apex Dermatology*

"I've often found it difficult to coach my teams in, and even leverage for myself, opportunities for growth that are more abstract and less tangible. Instead of creating an esoteric manifesto, Rick and Amy Simmons are offering a field guide equipped with definitive language and practical guidance on how to maximize the threshold seasons life presents and how to embrace, seek, and even curate those opportunities for ourselves. Their book is an open doorway for people and professionals at every level to seize the opportunity to grow purposefully through our circumstances, and not just accidentally or in spite of them. I highly recommend listening to what they have to say."

—**Thomas A. Haught,** *CFP®, ChFC®, President, Sequoia Financial Group*

"Rick and Amy deliver a powerful concept for leaders at all levels in an organization—learn to become 'comfortable feeling uncomfortable' while leveraging opportunities for positive change. Embrace these moments to communicate your vision, what's in it for your employees, and confidently lead your team towards the holy grail of 'esprit de corps.' I read it in one sitting and shared the next day with my leadership team. A must-read for all leaders who desire continued growth and development for themselves and their organizations."

—**Jim O'Rourke,** *Chief Procurement Officer, The Vanguard Group, Inc.*

"Amidst a period of true liminality in the healthcare industry, *Unleashed* offers us a roadmap forward, one grounded in resilience and agility, rooted in reality, and enabling equally all that's possible. A brilliant book!"

—**Cliff A. Megerian,** *MD, CEO, University Hospitals Health System*

"This is a must-read for anyone who is, or aspires to be, a change agent for the betterment of human systems. Those who excel in the helping professions or in facilitative roles ultimately realize that the self is your greatest instrument for change. In *Unleashed*, the authors model this by sharing their internal journeys to develop themselves to be better vehicles for positive change in others. Along their learning expeditions they discover liminality—that 'in between' space where one is separated from the comfortable, normal, or status quo and at the cusp of a yet-to-be-understood transformation. As a long-time fan of Victor Turner's work on the characteristics and dynamics of liminal states in indigenous cultural rituals of passage, I applaud Rick and Amy's work here to bring this concept forward into the domains of individual, organizational, and societal growth and development.

They aptly demonstrate through narratives and case examples how an appreciation for, and understanding of, liminality can produce what Turner called *communitas*—a relatively emergent collective state based on equality, solidarity, and generative connectedness, which is often at odds with the prior, normative social (group, organization, or communal) structure. We learn only when our current boundaries are in question, when we are at the edge of our comfort zones. *Unleashed* gives us new language, new questions, and new perspectives to help lean into these spaces of unknowing with confidence and hope."

—**Ronald Fry,** *PhD, Professor of Organizational Behavior, Case Western Reserve University*

"The introduction to the concept of liminal space through Rick and Amy has allowed me to view tough situations through the lens of growth and development rather than problems. My growth as a leader and a person has been exponential as my understanding of liminality has developed, allowing me to share this with my coaching clients with wonderful results."

—**Chris Nagel,** *Senior Director, Organization and Leadership Development*

"We all worry too much about things that have happened in the past and/or what will happen in the future, when all of our focus should really be on living in the present. Rick and Amy's book exemplifies how living in the present allows one to see more clearly and stay focused on and take advantage of opportunities that are present to us."

—**Marc Stefanski,** *CEO, Third Federal Savings and Loan*

RICK SIMMONS & AMY SIMMONS

unleashed.

Harnessing the Power of Liminal Space

ForbesBooks

Published by ForbesBooks, Charleston, South Carolina.
Member of Advantage Media Group.

ForbesBooks is a registered trademark, and the ForbesBooks colophon is a trademark of Forbes Media, LLC.

Printed in the United States of America.

10 9 8 7 6 5 4 3 2 1

ISBN: 978-1-95086-313-6
LCCN: 2021903271

Cover design by David Taylor.
Layout design by Wesley Strickland.

 Advantage Media Group is proud to be a part of the Tree Neutral® program. Tree Neutral offsets the number of trees consumed in the production and printing of this book by taking proactive steps such as planting trees in direct proportion to the number of trees used to print books. To learn more about Tree Neutral, please visit www.treeneutral.com.

Since 1917, Forbes has remained steadfast in its mission to serve as the defining voice of entrepreneurial capitalism. ForbesBooks, launched in 2016 through a partnership with Advantage Media Group, furthers that aim by helping business and thought leaders bring their stories, passion, and knowledge to the forefront in custom books. Opinions expressed by ForbesBooks authors are their own. To be considered for publication, please visit www.forbesbooks.com.

To Kyle, Quinn, Maddie, and Zoë, our most treasured companions on our journey through liminal space

leadership foundation.

WE'LL ALWAYS NEED LEADERS.
WE'RE STARTING EARLY.

The telos Leadership Foundation was established by telos's founding partners to provide transformational leadership development opportunities for young people of all backgrounds. The fund, managed by The Cleveland Foundation, will deliver programs proven to help young people develop into positive, emotionally and socially aware leaders.

A portion of the proceeds from this book will be used to support the telos Leadership Foundation's efforts.

contents.

authors' note.

We would be remiss if we did not acknowledge the environment in which this text was written. As of this writing, we face a set of unprecedented circumstances—the likes of which few, if any, of us have seen in our lifetimes.

The novel coronavirus and the disease it causes, COVID-19, have sent the world into a tailspin. With the shutdown of schools and "non-essential" businesses around the globe, markets have become volatile, and economies and families are struggling to keep up. And as many organizations begin to reopen without a viable vaccine, people are finding themselves choosing between their livelihood and their health.

Further, the virus and its disproportionate impact on underserved communities and people of color—as well as increased attention on inequity and police brutality in the US—have thrown into harsh relief long-standing societal injustices, particularly in America. By the same token, political partisanship seems to have reached an all-time high.

We find ourselves adrift in a sea of disruption, or liminal space, the subject of this book.

While the multitude of factors demanding that we reevaluate how we operate personally, professionally, and as a society may seem disparate, upon closer reflection, we can see the interconnectedness of these events. What we have on our hands is a chain reaction, catalyzed in large part by a common foe: a virus we have never seen before.

But perhaps more important, alongside great challenge and even devastation lie immense opportunities. There are myriad benefits to such periods of discontinuity, times that force us to reflect on what we have, what we've lost, what we want—and what is possible.

Regardless of when you are reading it, with this book, we aim to equip you with the tools to access those benefits. After all, when harnessed to one's advantage, adversity—and wading into the unknown—can pave the way to transformation.

foreword.

I only wish I had the benefit of reading *Unleashed: Harnessing the Power of Liminal Space* while I was running large businesses for a global professional services firm. I often witnessed business executives across the globe wasting opportunities to drive change and frankly live happier, more fulfilled lives. Instead, they were overwhelmed by the velocity of events they faced every day. *Unleashed* provides an escape hatch from that vicious cycle. It is truly a gift for those who want to take control of their lives.

Rick Simmons and Amy Simmons first introduced me to the concept of liminal space more than five years ago. I was intrigued, but initially I believed it to be a theoretical notion that would be challenging to apply in a practical manner.

Soon, I understood that liminality boils down to something far simpler: How we handle change can make or break our lives and careers.

The telos institute is well known for its Leadership Ventures to remote locations such as Patagonia, the Grand Canyon, and Iceland. Ventures take participants out of their comfort zone and place them in "liminal space," which triggers breakthrough thinking. After learning about the impact of these treks, my challenging question to Rick and Amy was, "How can I put myself in liminal space at home or in the office—environments in which I have limited time and resources to embrace change, seize the day, and put my brain into overdrive?"

In *Unleashed*, Rick and Amy teach readers how to do just that. They share real-life examples from their organizational development practice to drive home the many ways in which individuals can harness life experiences they cannot control—from the tragedy of losing a loved one, to a promotion into an intimidating role—and those they trigger themselves for transformation.

Over the years as a strategic advisor to telos, I have witnessed the journey Rick, Amy, and their team of professionals have been on to bring liminality to life. They have developed the concepts illuminated in *Unleashed* through brainstorming sessions with leading professionals, workshops with clients, and the interrogation of their personal experiences. I have utilized their concepts and coaching personally and know first-hand the liberating impact of shifting my perspective to view some of life's most daunting events as catalysts for change.

As I write this, in January of 2021, COVID-19 has changed so much in our world. Who would have imagined coming into 2020 that the paradigm of winners and losers in various industries would be turned upside down? Factors like how we work, how we interact, where we wish to live, and more have changed substantially in less than twelve months. While the pandemic will pass, the current construction of our society ensures that we will continue to experience rapid change in our personal and professional worlds. Whenever you are reading, and whatever your goals, *Unleashed* will prepare you for success—however you define it.

—Bryan Segedi, *Retired Vice Chairman, Ernst & Young*

acknowledgments.

Our path to discovering, exploring, and operationalizing liminal space—and to sharing what we've learned with you in this book—has been shaped by so many teachers, fellow students, colleagues, mentors, friends, and family, only a fraction of whom we have named here.

We are indebted to them for generously offering us a window into their minds and hearts, and for seeing the value in ours.

We are eternally grateful to our classmates and professors at the Weatherhead School of Management at Case Western Reserve University. Special thanks to Dr. Ron Fry, Dr. Eric Neilsen, Dr. David Cooperider, and the members of our MOD XV Class. To Johan Hovelynck, professor at Katholieke Universiteit Leuven, who first introduced us to the verbiage that would ultimately shape our organization and purpose. To Dr. Margaret Brooks-Terry, Dr. Greg Pett, Mary Garton, and Marian Hancy, thank you for believing in us at formative points in our personal and professional lives.

To the team at ForbesBooks: Adam Witty, Keith Kopcsak, Bree Barton, Kristin Goodale, Nate Best, and everyone else who helped usher *Unleashed* to publication. Your support and encouragement throughout the process has meant a great deal. Special thanks to Ariel Hubbard whose curiosity, patience, and enthusiasm helped us find our liminal voice.

To all of our many friends who have touched our lives deeply. Special thanks to Dan and Meghan Latham, Jim and Kelly Laudato, Kristen and Mark Kolar, Brian Brennan, Kim Wagner, Shelley Vilardo, Andy Edgar, Bryan Wadsworth, Jeff Zeiger, Joe Glick, Matt Pullar, and Amanda Quijano. We so appreciate our enduring bond.

To our colleagues at the telos institute, we quite literally couldn't do it without you. To Bryan Segedi and Al Weiss, your guidance and counsel throughout our professional expedition has been invaluable. To telos's numerous external supporters—particularly Scott Cundy and all our friends at Wildland Trekking, the members of our Scientific Advisory Board, and Mark Davis—you too are a crucial part of our team.

To our clients who have trusted us with your greatest dreams, challenges, unique opportunities, and your own precious liminal experiences, it has truly been an honor to be part of your journey; we do not take your partnership for granted.

Finally, to our parents for providing a foundation for our growth. To our siblings for supporting our journey. And to our children, Kyle, Quinn, Maddie, and Zoe, for being some of the very best teachers we've ever had.

"In the universe, there are things that are known and things that are unknown, and in between them, there are doors."

—William Blake

introduction.

In today's hyperconnected world, we're inundated with invitations to strive for more, reach for who we truly are, and evolve into our most authentic selves. We're deluged with instructions on how to tap into our greatest "intelligence"—emotional, social, conversational, or otherwise. Individuals and organizations alike are compelled to discover our *why*, with the hope of establishing a strong foundation for all we are and all we do, one that will eventually lead to incredible success. Entire industries have developed around that goal, with experts in a range of fields imploring us to explore our *who*, *what*, and *how* in order to determine that *why*. As executive coaches and consultants, we're very familiar with this pursuit and the typical efforts that go along with it.

But what if the answer to our *why* actually lies in our *when*? What if *when* we exist on the continuum of our journey holds the key to harnessing our greatest opportunities for change, growth, and development? What if we discovered that there are inflection points along our paths as individuals, teams, entire organizations, and even societies that can pave the way for transformative course corrections, thereby accelerating us in the direction of our best selves?

We call these periods *liminal space*.

These inflection points occur in nature at different periods in any particular life cycle. Anything and everything—trees, children, businesses—grows in a stair-step pattern. It shoots up, levels off, and shoots up again. If you pan back far enough, the process looks like a straight line. But no living system grows like that; all of them experience disruptions along the way. And it's those very disruptions that lead to more growth.

You've no doubt been shaped by those moments. Everyone has experienced periods of discontinuity—a parent passing away, the end of a relationship, the loss of a job, the challenge of navigating a foreign situation or environment. While these events may be difficult or even devastating to face, they can lead to powerful transformation, *locating previously untapped ideas, strengths, and solutions that have the potential to catapult you to new heights personally and professionally*. Much of that power lies in your ability to identify liminal space—*those inevitable periods of change or instability—and use them as opportunities for growth*.

In fact, it was when we first put a name to those inflection points that we were able to see their incredible potential. We met pursuing our master's degrees in organizational behavior. Little did we know we'd not only become partners in work and life but also discover language for something we had experienced but never quite been able to label.

As part of our graduate program, we traveled abroad to Belgium to spend several weeks at a sister university. There, we visited companies, heard case studies, engaged in simulations, and more. Everyone on the trip was struck by how much we were learning. In just a few days, we had grown and changed tremendously. When Amy shared what she had been experiencing with Johann, our Belgian professor, he responded with a shrug, "Well, this is a liminal space." That simple phrase became the basis of our work.

Having a term for it was eye opening, to say the least. We came away from that program wanting to give others the opportunity to explore and grow from liminal space, because our time spent there had such a profound impact on our lives. We came up with the idea for our organization, the telos institute, on the plane ride home. We didn't have the name yet, or all the pieces, but we knew that helping people access these kinds of experiences would be at the heart of our work.

You don't have to go to Belgium to harness the power of liminal space (though it certainly helps). These inflection points are all around us. Think, for a moment, about the sun. For so long, we've been ignoring the fact that the sun is an incredible power source and have instead relied on fossil fuels. Meanwhile, we have a tremendous source of energy that is virtually at our fingertips; we just have to tap into it. Liminal space works similarly. It's a remarkable catalyst for productive change. It's just a matter of recognizing it, acknowledging its potential value, and using it to make meaningful progress.

Most people don't realize they're at an inflection point. They just know something is out of alignment.

But therein lies the rub. In the years we've spent studying liminal space and its influence on people and organizations, we've learned that *most people don't realize they're at an inflection point. They just know something is out of alignment.*

It's akin to going to the doctor for a particular ailment. You may be able to point to your head or your knee and say, "It hurts here." But frequently, the cause and the symptom don't originate from the same locale. That headache could be caused by eyestrain, and the problem with your knee may be due to tightness in your hips. Or—as is frequently the case—those aches and pains could be indicators of a systemic issue.

In our work, we often see organizations struggle to come up with the correct diagnosis. They may believe they have an issue with personnel, for instance. They think training someone up or hiring someone else will solve it, but more often than not, it's a bigger-picture issue. What appears to be a people problem may actually be evidence that the organization has entered liminal space. And the right diagnosis can be invaluable in helping them get from here to there.

Here's an example. A client in the healthcare industry once told us, "We have a people problem in the lab." But when we came in, we discovered that there was a greater challenge afoot. Over the past three or four years, a number of people had retired. Others had gone on maternity leave and never returned. Each time someone left, their reports were directed to one individual—we'll call her Ellen. By the time we arrived, Ellen was overseeing eighty-five people. As you might imagine, she was running into some difficulties. Employees felt their needs weren't being met, and things were slipping through the cracks.

But this wasn't a people problem. Ellen was a good employee who had been put in a bad spot. She wasn't receiving the support or attention she needed and was thus struggling to meet unrealistic demands. Meanwhile, the real sticking point was that the organization was in liminal space. People had left. New people had yet to be hired. There was the way things worked yesterday, the way they'd work tomorrow, and the in-between point. That's where this particular client was—smack-dab in liminal space.

But because this organization didn't understand where they were on the continuum, they weren't able to identify what was going on. They were in a transition period: people had been leaving for years, and as a stopgap, they were directed to Ellen. But rather than realizing this and developing a new management structure, the organization let it simply become the way things worked. No one acknowledged the temporary condition as an opportunity to develop something better. They just pressed on, with no vision of the after.

And without the awareness that they were in liminal space, they imagined their challenges must stem from personality or communication skills or experience or intellect, rather than recognizing that the friction they were experiencing was simply due to the fact that they had reached a crossroads. But once we helped the organization identify the point in time they were on the continuum, they were able to address the issues they were having, make real progress, and cut poor Ellen a break. The company learned that when they could recognize that they were in liminal space, they could leverage that period for systematic organizational betterment.

But there's another piece to this puzzle. Back when we first learned about liminal space, we began wondering if we had to sit around and wait for those inflection points—those periodic earthquakes that arrive in our lives and spur us to reevaluate—to benefit from the kind of disruption they create.

We set out to help participants unleash the power of liminal space and liberate greatness for themselves, their teams, and their organizations.

What would a curated period of disruption look like? Could you incubate these periods on your own—creating tremors that would not bring down the house but shake things up enough to become open to new considerations? That's what led us to develop the telos institute's first offering: telos Leadership Ventures. Through leadership development experiences that invite participants to test their edges to drive personal and professional change, we set out to help participants unleash the power of liminal space and liberate greatness for themselves, their teams, and their organizations. Since then, we've added additional coaching and development opportunities that capture the nontraditional spirit of our ventures. Both help people and organizations cultivate productive disruption and ultimately catalyze their own success. We want you to have the same opportunity. Consider this your guide.

Unleashed will help you not only leverage the liminal space you find yourself in—including challenging situations you never wanted or asked for—but actually *create* inflection points that will transform your business, relationships, and life.

Just to be clear, this is more than just an intellectual exercise; we've lived it. This book is born of our own inflection points, both personally and professionally. We've felt the impact of being aware that we were in a transitional period: moments of uncertainty and discomfort that, when harnessed, helped us accomplish incredible things, many of which we couldn't have imagined previously. But to achieve those results, we had to recognize and name what we were experiencing—and capitalize on it. That's what we'll help you do here.

In these pages, we'll

- explain why these periods are so ripe with opportunity,

- share how to best leverage key points of inflection,

- reveal real-life examples of when liminal space was best managed for transformative results, and

- provide insight on how to thoughtfully trigger and curate these moments on your own.

And while we'll provide a new language and framework to enable growth, the concept of liminal space itself is valuable in its simplicity. You can apply it immediately, stepping away from the first chapter with tools to be more thoughtful and deliberate about how to optimize any transition.

As we often tell the executives we work with, when it comes to increasing your leadership capacity, *you* are the most valuable lever you have. Thus, any work you do to grow your understanding of these transitions will be wildly beneficial, improving your ability to reach your goals—whatever they may be. With all that in mind, join us on a journey to unleash the power of liminal space.

CHAPTER 1

what is liminal space?

Rick had lost track of time and space. The sky was dark, an inky black that faded to bruise blue at the horizon line, but he wasn't sure whether that meant morning was fast approaching or the day before was still in retreat. He was in an ultramarathon, the goal of which was to run as many miles as possible in twenty-four hours. He had trained and prepared. He had the diet down and the race plan in place, and he had gathered together a group of family and friends to serve as his crew.

Every hour, Amy would appear by his side, and he would slow down for a moment to eat something while she asked him a series of five questions:

- What's your goal?

- How are you feeling?

- What are you thinking about?

- What's been most challenging since I last asked?

- What's been most helpful along the way?

He'd offer up his answers, and before he knew it, it felt like she was asking them again.

This time, it was hour twelve. *What's your goal?* For the first eleven hours of the race, it had been twenty-four and one hundred: to run for all twenty-four hours and go at least one hundred miles. But the day had been hotter than expected, and Rick was behind and feeling pretty dejected. His body was tense, his breath short, catching with each inhale. "What's your goal?" Amy asked.

In every previous hour, he had simply responded, "twenty-four and one hundred." But this time, rather than repeating what he'd stuck to all along, he said, "To be okay with me no matter how far I go."

He surprised himself with the answer. Right after he said it, he finally felt himself exhale. He had been gripping his goal, holding on to his progress—or lack thereof—so tightly. But in the moments that followed, he felt free to let the future unfold without trying to control it.

The shift was visible—Amy could actually see that "aha" moment, the physical change in Rick's being. His face relaxed, his shoulders loosened, and his gait lengthened. After that, he ran the next twelve hours significantly faster than the first twelve and exceeded that goal he had been so concerned with, without thinking much about it.

That period, where space and time had dissolved and Rick produced an answer—seemingly from thin air—gave him the freedom necessary to get where he needed to go. It allowed him to come to some serious conclusions that changed the trajectory of his personal and professional life.

He realized that whether you're raising a child or running an organization or completing something as silly as a twenty-four-hour footrace, you often get to this place where you're too far in to stop but not quite sure how in the hell it's all going to play out. You're nine months into a product launch. You can't stop now, but you really don't know what's going to happen. You've got a fourteen-year-old whose behavior feels like more than you can handle, but you certainly can't just quit parenting. Ultimately, you've got to keep watching to see how the movie ends. That uncertainty is the primary marker of liminal space, and it holds incredible potential.

Defining Liminal Space

The word *liminal* comes from the Latin word *līmen*, or "threshold." It is—quite literally—a point of transition, a space where what has happened in the past no longer applies and what will come hasn't yet arrived. We define liminal space as a period of discontinuity that creates an openness to change. To use the more universally accepted verbiage, an inflection point. For our purposes, *liminality*.

We define liminal space as a period of discontinuity that creates an openness to change.

Ethnographer and folklorist Arnold van Gennep first coined *liminality* to describe rites of passage, ceremonies and rituals that have been a part of human existence since its origins. Faith traditions have marked transitional moments in a person's life for thousands of years, from birth through death. The rhythm of life as a young person also has natural transitions built into it—from school to summer and back again. They become circadian in a way; we get used to them. But after we've finished our formal education, we're spit out into a void of sorts, one that is devoid of the same kinds of signals that used to come with that summertime shift. Those built-in phases that are an inherent part of our early lives oftentimes completely vanish later on.

Many of the transitional markers that were once woven into the fabric of our society are being lost too. The world is trending more secular, with religious traditions being left by the wayside. In many areas, school is extending into summer, shedding that transition between one year and the next. We are just letting those rites of passage go. As a result, we miss the chance to reflect, assess, and envision.

Without a way to recognize those periods, when we're faced with big life events—the death of a loved one, an illness, a move—we don't know what to do. We've lost the capacity to effectively deal with and manage these moments and, perhaps most important, use them as catalysts for change.

But when you recognize that there's power in that in-between—that discontinuity creates an openness to transformation—you can do something about it. You have the opportunity to build a new reality rather than just struggling to return to normal. Not long ago, the head of talent at a nationwide healthcare system finished one of our development experiences and immediately shared that the concept of liminal space was one of the top takeaways he'd encountered in his entire professional career. Simply knowing that he could identify that he, his team, and his organization were at an inflection point allowed him to understand why they were all feeling a sense of vertigo and uncertainty—and move forward. Being able to define it and name it has been a liberating component for many of the people and companies we've worked with.

As far as definitions go, few have put it better than Richard Rohr, an author and theologian who described the vast potential of liminal space as "where we are betwixt and between the familiar and the completely unknown. There alone is our old world left behind, while we are not yet sure of the new existence. That's a good space where genuine newness can begin. Get there often and stay as long as you can by whatever means possible ... This is the sacred space where the old world is able to fall apart, and a bigger world is revealed. If we don't encounter liminal space in our lives, we start idealizing normalcy. The threshold is God's waiting room. Here we are taught openness and patience as we come to expect an appointment with the divine Doctor."[1]

And the good news is that liminality is all around us.

The Doorway Effect

Here's a scenario that may be familiar: You're sitting in the living room of your home when you remember a task that needs tending to in the kitchen. But when you cross the threshold from one room to the next, you can no longer remember what you needed to do. It's a common phenomenon, one that a team of researchers—led by the University of Notre Dame's Gabriel Radvansky—studied at length. They called it the "Location Updating Effect," though you may know it as the "Doorway Effect."[2]

Theories abound as to what exactly is happening during these times. Radvansky noted that memories are often stored in discreet episodes and that leaving the room signals the end of that episode, clearing the decks for a new memory. Others have pointed to an evolutionary explanation. In our cave-dwelling days, predators liked to lurk at the edge of clearings. That way, they could remain hidden in

---

1   "What Is A Liminal Space?" Liminal Space, https://inaliminalspace.org/about-us/
     what-is-a-liminal-space/.

2   G. Radvansky, A. K. Tamplin, and S. A. Krawietz, "Walking Through Doorways Causes
     Forgetting: Environmental Integration," *Psychonomic Bulletin and Review,* December
     17, 2010 (6):900-4. doi: 10.3758/PBR.17.6.900.

thick vegetation but still see clearly across all that open space, allowing them to spot prey while avoiding dangers themselves. Early humans could have certainly adapted to focus on their surroundings and let everything else go when crossing such thresholds. The Doorway Effect could have acted as a sort of wake-up call, directing attention away from internal musings and on to external reality.

Whatever its origins, the Doorway Effect remains a part of our consciousness, and thresholds of all sizes present opportunities to refocus and make the most of that transitional opportunity. With so many of these liminal opportunities arising all the time, you're almost guaranteed to be in one of them now yourself or closely related to someone who is experiencing one.

However, while liminal space is all around us, it's not always available in equal measure. There are long periods in that stair-step growth model where we're just bumping along, without a significant opportunity to make real change. It's important to recognize that and avoid going down the rabbit hole of believing that everything is liminal space. Creating disruption every day for the sake of disruption is misguided and ill-advised. All it will beget is chaos. Instead, it's about knowing *when* to lean in to either curate disruption or respond effectively to it that makes all the difference.

What Does Liminal Space Feel Like?

So, how do you know when you're really in liminal space? There's a break in the pattern, a sense of discomfort. You're feeling out of sorts, and most likely you don't know why. Your business may be experiencing some disruption—expected or not. But typically, there's a reason for it. For example, we talk a lot about the telos levers of organizational performance—purpose, people, product, process, and performance—which must be aligned for optimal functioning. These areas are rarely static, and as they shift, we often see another concept at play: threes and tens. The idea is that when you reach a tipping point in any of these four areas—going from thirty people to 100 people; three products to ten; a process involving three decisions to one that requires ten of them; $30 million to $100 million in revenue—everything needs to be reimagined. It's almost like clockwork. We'll sit down with an organizational leader who feels things shifting under their feet without any discernable rhyme or reason only to find that they just hit a new milestone in size or revenue.

It's not only on the upswing that liminality arises; things may be heading downward too. Or that out-of-sorts feeling may be tied to something you can easily point to, a transition in leadership—a change that is identifiable and/or measurable. You find yourself somewhere between what it used to be but not yet at what it will become. There may be recognition of the incongruence between daily life and larger ambitions, a set of values, or an overarching mission. All of these are signals that you've reached a crossroads, a powerful point on your continuum, be it personal or professional. And to make progress, you may have to embrace that discomfort.

(Adversity + Reflection) x Action = Growth and Progress

Every year we bring together telos clients and staff from around the world. It's curated liminal space for the telos institute: three days where we have the opportunity to shape and grow our organization for the coming year—bringing in new thoughts and ideas and creating a lab of sorts, where we can experiment with different ideas and take them to our clients moving forward.

In 2019, we convened a dinner for eighteen C-suite leaders. We asked each of them to bring with them a story of a time in their careers that led to their ascension to the top.

After the appetizers arrived, the first person stood up. They told a story of adversity, how they had been knocked all the way down and how working through that moment enabled them to rise back up—better and stronger than before. For the next hour and a half, we heard seventeen more stories of people stumbling and failing their way forward—reaching a pinnacle that few of them could have pictured before they got tripped up.

The next morning, we got a text message from one of the participants. It read "The things I've tried to pretend away and avoid my whole career were in fact the very experiences that led me to the top." His takeaway? Adversity plus reflection, multiplied by action, equals growth and progress.

The way we proceed during troubling times dictates what happens next.

When we all look back, we realize that it was that stub of the toe or slip on the path or roadblock along our typical route that forced us to change course and ultimately led us to something bigger and better than we had been approaching before. But key to reaching new heights is how we manage that period of disruption. The way we proceed during troubling times dictates what happens next.

What to Do When You're Dropped behind Enemy Lines

What do you do if you think you might be in liminal space? We can turn to the Navy Seals for some insight. In basic training, they are taught to ask themselves three questions if and when they are dropped behind enemy lines (talk about being in liminal space!):

- Where am I?

- Where's the enemy?

- Where's my buddy?

It's no surprise to us that the goal of the first question is to locate oneself. Are you seven miles behind enemy lines, or just seven hundred yards past it? When you're feeling totally disoriented, being able to determine your exact location can help you establish some firm footing.

It can also grant you permission to be a bit disorganized. When you're in liminal space, you're dealing with a degree of chaos, and you must give yourself license to be there in the moment. Not everything has to line up at right angles, and expecting that to be the case won't help. For people who really appreciate right angles, it's really helpful to know that, by definition, this period is going to be marred with a little bit of messiness. That realization in and of itself can be pretty liberating.

Meanwhile, knowing *where* the enemy is located is as much about being clear about *whom* or *what* the enemy is. In life, it's easy to imagine there are enemies around every corner, but that's rarely the case. When you understand what you're truly up against, you can identify solutions to address it directly, instead of firing indiscriminately.

Locating your buddy is all about your reason for being. In the Navy, being alive helps your buddy stay alive as well. Whether your buddy in this particular case is your friend, a group of family members, or the business you helm, understanding where they are on the continuum in relation to your own position can help you both make it through in one piece.

With that in mind, let's talk a little bit more about what liminal space can look like, and the vast potential it holds. In the next chapter, we'll take a deep dive into a key liminal period experienced by one of the world's greatest tech leaders, as well as our own transformative dive into liminal space.

CHAPTER 2

our wilderness experience.

Steve Jobs needs no introduction. His story, swathed in his signature black turtleneck, is the stuff of legends. But most people focus on Apple's origin story, or on act one, and the third act, which was Jobs's triumphant return to transform the struggling company into the incredible tech phenomenon it is today. They don't explore—or don't know—what happened in between.

Back in the mid-eighties, Apple was struggling, failing to pull in the earnings it expected. By then, Steve Jobs was a world-renowned success. But in 1985, the company went through a reorganization, and Jobs was ousted from his position. He had started his company at just twenty-one, become a millionaire by twenty-three, and then—at thirty—it seemed as if it might all be over. "What had been the focus of my entire adult life was gone, and it was devastating ... I was a very public failure," he told Stanford's class of 2005 in his commencement speech.[3] With that, he was launched into what the media would dub

---

3   Steve Jobs, "Commencement Speech," Stanford University, Palo Alto, CA, June 12, 2005, https://news.stanford.edu/news/2005/june15/jobs-061505.html.

his "wilderness experience"—a period of trial and error, small successes and bigger failures, during which Jobs tried to find his footing.

During his time away from Apple, Jobs founded NeXT to develop a computer that would serve the higher-education market. But prices were much higher than Apple's McIntosh, and universities weren't biting. When that didn't work, he tried to sell the product to corporations at an even higher rate. That was a flop too. After seven years (and with only fifty thousand computers sold), he stopped production on the machines themselves and focused on selling software. Eventually, Apple acquired NeXT, modeling its new operating system on the company's software, and Steve came back to run things. You no doubt know the rest of the story.[4]

So, was firing Steve Jobs a big mistake on the part of Apple's board, one that was blessedly rectified when he was invited to take the reins again? Quite the opposite. It was his time away from the company—that "wilderness experience"—that made him the remarkable leader the world came to know, as author and Silicon Valley expert Randall Stross attests. "The Steve Jobs who returned to Apple was a much more capable leader—precisely because he had been badly banged up. He had spent twelve tumultuous, painful years failing to find a way to make the new company profitable."[5]

Those twelve years were textbook liminal space—a period of discontinuity in which things weren't what they had been or what they would become. In that sense, Jobs's experience is actually quite relatable. It's not that we've all been pushed out of the multimillion-dollar companies we built, of course. Rather, we have all been in that unique kind of limbo that those life-changing wilderness experiences

---

4   Randall Stross, "What Steve Jobs Learned in the Wilderness," New York Times, October 2, 2010. https://www.nytimes.com/2010/10/03/business/03digi.html.

5   Stross, "What Steve Jobs Learned."

impose. And what we can take from Jobs's story is this: it's not just having these experiences but what you choose to do with them that matters. Jobs didn't hole up in his thirty-room mansion and shake his fist at the world or move to a small island and take a very early retirement; he decided to move forward. He founded another company. He even had the awareness to name that company "Next." His act two was marked by trial and error, failures, and more, and he ultimately succeeded in the third act not in spite of but because of the challenges that second act brought.

Whether or not you've labeled it as such, you've undoubtedly had liminal experiences that drove you to positive action, action that allowed you to successfully change course and thrive, either personally or professionally. Those liminal experiences will continue to show up in your life. And whether you choose them or they choose you, each of those experiences begins with a catalytic moment that thrusts you into liminal space—an emotional upset or uplift that results in a transformational change. Our biggest one came in graduate school, in the Organizational Behavior program at Case Western's Weatherhead School of Management, where we met and ultimately redesigned our lives to pursue a new reality.

Our Wilderness Experience

Amy thought everything in her life was fine—maybe even the best it could be. She had done everything she was supposed to do and done it well. She had gone to college, graduated, found a job, gotten married, had kids. She was moving along. Graduate school seemed to provide an opportunity to advance all those aspects of her life, to do it all a little better, rather than to make systemic change. But she would realize she was playing more of a role than she thought. All the things she had worked so hard to achieve—the things she had thought were the best they could be—weren't making her whole. She had allowed life to happen to her. She would eventually decide to embark on a common experience: transitioning away from societal expectations to locate and embrace what she truly wanted.

Rick, on the other hand, was deliberately seeking change. He was unsatisfied with his job, and he thought that pursuing a graduate degree in organizational behavior would be a path that could provide more fulfillment. But nothing in his life was really broken. He, like Amy, was married with two young children. He was gainfully employed and had achieved an existence that was respectable by all external accounts. But he was living a life that was running counter-current to what was most important and meaningful to him, and that created tremendous subsurface pain. The effects of that dissonance were not so explicit that the outside world could see it, and on some level, that made it hurt worse. And while he knew he was uncomfortable and unhappy with the way things were, he certainly didn't realize that making the choice to attend graduate school would cause him to reflect on every aspect of his existence.

But indeed, in the years to come, both of us would take our worlds down to the rafters and mindfully rebuild our lives—piece by piece. At the time, we weren't familiar with the poem titled "The Summer Day," by Mary Oliver, but we certainly knew the essence of her question. And we knew that we wanted a better answer.

AN EXCERPT FROM *THE SUMMER DAY* BY MARY OLIVER

Tell me, what else should I have done?
Doesn't everything die at last, and too soon?
Tell me, what is it you plan to do
With your one wild and precious life?

In graduate school, we both saw new ideas and concepts come to life; we made friends and colleagues who allowed us to open up in ways we hadn't before. We were entering liminal space, though we didn't know it at the time. Our program served as a multiyear opportunity to pull out each facet of our lives, twist in the sunlight, and think about the selves we wanted to reflect. We had each been feeling numb, but with the sunlight reflecting through the facets of our existence—mental, emotional, financial, physical, and more—like a prism, we were able to see what life *could* be like. To get there, however, we'd have to shatter many of the trappings of our current existence.

We each checked off a fair number of the most pivotal moves that one can make in life during those years, both professionally and personally. Our passion for organizational development and our unwillingness to let go of a job done poorly brought us together, and we began reevaluating the careers and home lives we had built to date. After deep consideration, we decided to go into business with each other. We also embarked on another pivotal experience together: we both made the choice to step away from our respective relationships and become partners in all ways. It wasn't an easy—or linear—process by any means. There was certainly challenge and turmoil involved, but ultimately, we knew it was the right course.

From the outside, it might be easy to say, "What the hell were you thinking?" But we had taken the immersive experience we had been given—one that had turned our worlds upside down in so many ways—and applied a tremendous amount of self-awareness and reflection to it to determine our next steps. We used our *when* to chart our *what, how,* and *where* and, of course, our *why* and to do so explicitly. While to others it may have seemed that we were making a series of rash decisions, they were anything but. Instead, they were some of the most mindful and deliberate moves we had ever made.

The process of breaking our worlds down to rebuild them involved some uncertainty, however. To launch telos, we broke every entrepreneurial rule in the book. We burned the boats and quit our jobs at the outset. Even those who know us well probably thought we had more of a financial cushion than we did. But there was no soft landing in sight. With zero income, we had no choice but to make this work—a deliberate decision in and of itself. Still, we almost went bankrupt, draining all but a few thousand dollars of our retirement savings before things turned.

Of course, we couldn't convey that image to potential clients. We walked into every meeting with a professional, prosperous face. It wasn't an attempt to be disingenuous. We knew businesses wanted to do business with people who had it all together, and that's what we had to project. But during late nights at home, we just stared at the computer screen, working on proposals and wondering where the money was going to come from. At the time, we had four young children. When a client's check was on its way, we would wait for the mail to arrive. There were times when we had to make decisions about which bills to pay or what to get at the grocery store.

We'll always remember the turning point. We had virtually drained the retirement account and maxed out our credit cards. And we had just sent out a proposal that we had agonized over because it was for more money than we had ever asked for from a client. For days, we wondered if it was too much or not enough. We pondered whether, given our situation, we should cut the amount back just to make sure they'd take it. But in the end, we sent it off with the number we felt it was worth. It's hard to describe the relief we felt when they accepted. That allowed us to keep going.

Navigating the Wilderness

We're happy to report that we've exceeded where we had been financially, physically, emotionally, and more—even in the best of situations. But we realize that not every story ends up that way. Smart, talented people follow their dreams all the time and do go bankrupt or end up facing tremendous challenges or outright failure. We're not here to tell you it will all work out—regardless of how intentional you are in pursuing a new path—because that's just not always the case. However, it is possible to increase the likelihood that whatever course of action you take is moving you in the right direction—that it has the potential to get you where you want to go. Maybe launching a full-service gift-basket business sounds like a good idea, and it seems to align with what will make you happy. But if you can be thoughtful and deliberate about it, you can determine whether it's really the right decision. You can stress test it.

We decided we'd rather fail having tried it than always wonder if we could have done it.

Even though we didn't have a trust fund or cushion to count on if things didn't go our way, we had thoroughly stress-tested our idea. We decided we'd rather fail having tried it than always wonder if we could have done it. That remains our measure today.

At this point, our professional environment is different; the bets we're making are not all or nothing.

But when we're considering whether to invest in something from a business standpoint, we always ask ourselves if we'd rather blow it all up or not try at all. One of our colleagues likes to say, "It has to be a hell yes, or it's a no." We wholeheartedly agree. Go all in or don't bother. But don't do that indiscriminately. And know that if you do move forward, it will likely have an impact on every aspect of your life.

A liminal experience typically affects multiple parts of the system—physical, mental, emotional, spiritual—and that was certainly the case for us. We were thinking about new and different things, creating something from scratch, managing the emotions inherent in building new relationships and letting go of others. As we carefully rearranged everything in our lives, we also realized that, with our decision to be together, our families would be experiencing liminal space themselves. Our children were going to grow up together, share a home, and spend time apart. With that in mind, we were incredibly deliberate in bringing them together—coordinating how they met and got to know each other.

We thoughtfully built new rituals, ones that didn't belong to our kids alone nor to us as individuals but to all of us. Liminal space provided the perfect opportunity to do that. At our wedding, we had a sand ceremony, in which each of us poured colored sand into a jar, the layers building on each other in a single vessel. Today, the jar is one of our most prized possessions because it represents our family coming together. Our anniversary became a marker of that, not just of our commitment to each other but also of our families becoming a single unit.

That liminal experience also gave our kids the opportunity to reevaluate various aspects of their lives—to decide who they wanted to be, what groups they wanted to hang out with, and how they wanted to show up in the world. One of our sons made a very purposeful choice when he moved from middle school to high school. Rather than being friends with everyone, he decided to invest his time and effort in developing meaningful relationships with just a few other kids, to let it be okay if someone didn't like him. Without the foundation of the deliberate approach we modeled as we worked to combine our lives, we're not sure he would have been aware that that was a choice he could make.

His situation demonstrates the fact that liminality doesn't have to stem from or inflict pain. His experience was positive, and it still came with its own new territory, a period of figuring it out. You might sell your business and find yourself navigating a very different set of complexities than those you faced previously, ones that arrive when you don't have any financial constraints. Interestingly, they may be just as challenging as those that arise in a darker period.

The Right Ingredients for Transformational Change

Liminal periods, in which we don't know our 'next,' are ubiquitous and inevitable. Each ushers in a new chapter of life and holds varying degrees of disruption. Often, it's easier to recognize liminal space in retrospect—noting the catalyst and corresponding changes that brought you to the next level—than it is to identify them as they are unfolding. *But if you can recognize them up front, those periods will be much more productive.*

When we think about liminality, we think about its existence in four quadrants: mental, emotional, physical, and spiritual (we define spiritual as living according to one's values, whether that's rooted in a faith tradition or some other kind of life-management system). Is being tested in one of those quadrants enough to consider oneself in liminal space, or does it require two or three? Is four too many, leading someone to shut down entirely, rather than reap the benefits of liminal space? We hold that experiencing challenge in two or three of the quadrants is the sweet spot—causing enough disruption to invite progress, yet not promote paralysis.

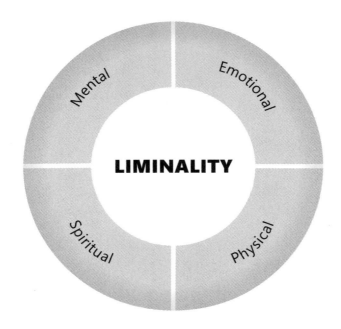

In addition to determining whether you're actually in liminal space, you must also figure out whether the circumstances are there to nurture powerful change. For example, one of the key factors to effectively moving through liminal space is a supportive community—a partner, dedicated friends, or a group of colleagues who have your back. But it's not just about having a cheerleading section; those people must bolster your ability to make necessary changes by challenging you too. Having that community allows you to make the decision to embrace your current station and continue to evolve. We've provided a list of some examples of liminality that will help determine whether you are in a period of liminal space and whether you have the resources to navigate it successfully—to move through at the right pace and harvest those periods of time more optimally.

LIMINALITY EXAMPLES

personal

> birth of child /grandchild
> "significant" birthday
> retirement
> move to a new city / home
> youngest child moves out
> divorce
> loss of a loved one
> serious illness (self or loved one)

professional

> job / career change
> promotion
> new team member / boss
> new product launch
> merger / acquisition
> deviation in business performance
> workplace relocation
> business exit

Finding Your Footing

While we can't prepare for every eventuality, we can stay flexible, nimble, and rhythmic in our assessment of our values and the direction we're going. That keeps us ready for those times when liminal moments arrive at our doorstep and puts us in a better position to move through them. And as the speed of societal change continues to accelerate at an ever-increasing rate, periods of liminality are coming faster and more frequently—and sometimes more violently—than they have previously. That means there's a greater opportunity to leverage this space than ever before.

Even more powerful, rather than waiting for liminal space to arrive, is the opportunity to create those moments, shaking the snow globe of your life personally and professionally to be able to iterate and improve in a more intentional way. Working in liminal space is like building a muscle. When you create it for yourself and you're able to harvest the power that comes from it, you can then build the skills and work with the tools to better manage it when it comes at you unexpectedly. There's a fitness level in dealing with those periods of discontinuity. If you're practiced in immersing yourself in liminal space, when those externally imposed disruptions happen—a death, a move, the end of a role—you're far more capable of handling them and using them to propel you to the next step.

In the next few chapters, we'll explore how *imposed* liminality—those periods that arrive on their own—presents for individuals, teams, and organizations, using real-life stories from clients and colleagues who were able to harness the power of liminal space to transform personally and professionally. Then, we'll dive into *curated* liminality: the concept that you can cultivate these periods of transformation for yourself. We'll begin our discussion of imposed liminality with a man whose entire life changed in a matter of moments.

CHAPTER 3

the value of vulnerability.

How Liminality Presents for Individuals

Dr. Julian Kim, a surgical oncologist, was at the top of his game. When Rick met him, he was participating in a physician leadership engagement with telos at University Hospitals in Cleveland, a cohort-driven experience with twenty-five of his colleagues. telos runs a number of these leadership engagements, helping highly competent technicians, whether they be in law, finance, technology, healthcare, or other domains, increase their effectiveness as leaders. That's what Dr. Kim was there to do. He had earned an international reputation for his skill as a physician and had taken on significant leadership responsibilities, helping to build University Hospitals' new Seidman Cancer Center, the only freestanding cancer hospital in the region, a 375,000-square-foot, state-of-the-art space centralizing all the hospital's cancer services under one roof. And then he had a stroke.

I was in the middle of surgery when the resident next to me noticed something. "You're dragging your foot a little," he said. "Do you think you could be having a stroke?" When I looked down, I noticed that he was right—my foot was tilted at a strange angle, kind of sideways. I was rushed to the neuro-intensive-care unit. I had had undiagnosed high blood pressure, which set off an intracranial bleed.

Afterward, I was in bed for a while. I couldn't move my left side, and I was entirely dependent on nurses to turn me, to get me up to go to the bathroom. Then, for eight weeks, I was in a wheelchair. I went through inpatient and outpatient therapy to start walking again.

When you're a patient, a lot of people come and wish you well. They spend time by your bedside. But eventually, everyone leaves your room, and you're left there, staring at the ceiling, wondering what's going to happen to your life. That was something I had never really experienced before. There had been times personally and professionally when I had dealt with challenges, of course, when I had to pause, take inventory, and make decisions, but this was the first time I'd ever really felt helpless, plagued by fear and doubt.

From a professional standpoint, I had reached the pinnacle of my career. I had far exceeded the expectations I had set for myself professionally. I had built a beautiful free-standing cancer hospital in Cleveland, where I served as chief medical officer. I had assembled a group of cancer surgeons who were some of the highest performers in our department. Everything was clicking, and in an instant, it was all in jeopardy.

Initially, my thoughts were about my family. Would they be okay? Then, I thought about how I would fare. I knew I wasn't going to be able to go back to surgery right away because I couldn't do much with my left side. But I was doing well cognitively, and I felt like I still had a lot to offer. I was staring down my current situation—just learning to walk—but my professional future also hung in the balance.

While I was out, I'd gotten a new supervisor. The first day I came back, my new boss told me, "You can't lead your surgical group if you can't operate." It was a punch to the gut. I had wanted them to tell me that they'd work to rehabilitate me and get me back in the operating room. Of course, I understood the business side of medicine, too, though that didn't make it any easier.

Instead of making the offer I had been hoping for, the hospital agreed to take me back as chief medical officer of the cancer hospital, an administrator. At the time, I was fifty-six, going on fifty-seven. I could have taken disability and retired. It certainly would have been justified. But the feeling that I still had more to give lingered. So, I decided to go back to work as chief medical officer and gave up the opportunity to stay on disability.

Even though I was happy in my role leading the cancer hospital, the fact that I wasn't doing surgery—which had been a big part of my life and my role there—made me feel as if I didn't have a long-term future with the organization. It certainly was no fault of the hospital's. The leadership team saw value in me; it was just a different value than the one I used to provide.

Things began to feel awkward. I'd go to work, do my job. But there were long periods of time when I would have been seeing patients—something I was not allowed to do until I recovered—or operating. They became hours that didn't quite have purpose.

During that time, I had a lot of conversations with my wife. Our daughter was in Cleveland, and she had just had a baby. We were going to have to decide whether we'd stay there—with me in my limited role—and continue on with our family life or whether we would open ourselves up to new opportunities, other situations elsewhere that might be a better fit for me.

As it turned out, I was offered an opportunity in South Carolina. The head of surgery at Prisma Health had been a friend of mine for many years, and the organization needed someone to help lead cancer surgery services in the region. He had hinted about me coming down there several times prior to my stroke, but I had always brushed it off. "I'm at the top of the world here; why would I go to South Carolina and start something new?" I'd tease. But now that I was looking at the world through a different lens, it seemed like a promising option.

I saw the opportunity as a chance to put a capstone on my career. I could work to change the way healthcare was delivered to an underserved patient population. In South Carolina, medicine hasn't quite reached the same level as it has in Cleveland. I thought I could make an impact.

When I came to South Carolina, the first person I met was the CEO. At that point, I was barely able to walk without a cane. "I have a great resume," I said, "but I'm a surgeon who can't operate. With all due respect, why are you even talking to me?"

His answer stuck with me. He was focused on my value as a leader, a visionary, someone who could change the way healthcare is being delivered to a large population of patients. None of it had anything to do with me performing an individual operation on a patient.

I gave it a lot of thought and decided that it was the right next step. I'm here in South Carolina today. I never would have expected to leave where I was and be where I am now. It's all a result of what I went through.

I came to a few powerful realizations through this experience. I recognized my own vulnerability. That's something I didn't feel much at all before my stroke. I was extremely confident—I felt like I could handle any situation that presented itself. But after my stroke, I realized I wasn't as infallible as I had thought and neither was anyone else. Organizations restructure, telling their senior leaders that they're simply going in a different direction. People get sick and can't work the way they used to. I also began to see the value in those experiences.

I had been at the top of the mountain, but when I got knocked down, I had the opportunity to recreate myself. The stroke I had was the most terrifying, humbling, and brutal experience I'd ever been through. I see everything differently now. I appreciate things I never would have noticed in the past.

> **I had been at the top of the mountain, but when I got knocked down, I had the opportunity to recreate myself.**

People see me differently too. I'm more accessible than I was before, with my suit and tie and perfect posture. During my recovery, total strangers would come up to me. "I see you every day, and I can see your progress. You just keep working," they'd tell me. My vulnerability opened the door for those interactions.

That vulnerability was bolstered by my experience working in high-functioning organizations in a different part of the country—Cleveland Clinic, Case Western Reserve University, University Hospitals—and it meant I had seen and experienced a lot of things that just haven't happened in this region yet. I would share my ideas, and they really seemed to resonate with people. Nine months after I arrived, the chief clinical officer for the local healthcare system departed. Soon after, I got a call from the CEO. He wanted me to consider taking on the role. At first, I didn't think I was the right choice. I had been there for less than a year. There were people who had been there for their entire careers, who knew the health system inside and out. When I asked him why he wanted me, he said, "Well, people like what you have to say."

It was a simple answer, but I think I've come to understand what he meant: they appreciated my humility, my willingness to listen.

Today, I still feel vulnerable; the organization is going through a restructuring. I've seen people who have been here for twenty years be relieved of their duties. What I've come to realize is that it's never over—you get over one hurdle, and the next one is standing right there, staring you in the face. Life is a continuous process of trying to overcome, to manage. But instead of panicking, I focus on what I can control, on getting through.

My stroke gave me perspective about my role on this earth. Having that perspective helps me realize that there's more to the world than my office, than trying to cut my budget or meet my bottom line. Right now, I'm sitting in an office with plaques all over the walls. Looking over them, I realize that life is what happens in between all that stuff.

Rick actually had a meeting scheduled with Dr. Kim right after he spoke with the new president at University Hospitals, when he was given the news that his role as a surgical oncologist was over. He'll never forget walking into Dr. Kim's office, seeing the blank look on his face just moments after being told that his reason for being as a professional was now in question. Dr. Kim had been thrust into liminal space, facing disruptive challenges physically, emotionally, and professionally. In times like these, it's natural to want to spend time thinking without making progress or vice versa—to trudge onward without giving much thought to where you're going. But those instincts have to be calibrated. That takes work. We helped him recognize what had happened, where he was, and the path forward both in terms of his recovery and his professional progress.

Fast-forward two years. Dr. Kim and his wife are resettled in South Carolina, where he is working to revolutionize the healthcare system there. The move had also given him the opportunity to reevaluate his priorities. Back when he first started working with Rick, Dr. Kim had shared that he and his wife had a second home in Hilton Head, but he felt they didn't get down there enough. Now, they are just a car ride away. The last time Rick and Dr. Kim spoke via video call, he and his wife were about to jump in the car to drive to Hilton Head for the weekend. His stroke was one of the most difficult experiences of his life, but in the period that followed, he was able to reflect on what was important, what wasn't, and how he wanted to prioritize those things in his next chapter.

It would have been easier for him to simply take the first job that was offered to him, to find something local, rather than disrupting the rest of his life. But after reflecting and assessing, he chose to do something different, with tremendous results. It goes back to the equation we shared in chapter 1, that adversity plus reflection, multiplied by action, equals growth and progress. He didn't just return to his previous status; he was propelled beyond the level he had reached before, in every area of his life.

The Value of Vulnerability

Dr. Kim also allowed for another factor key to successfully moving through liminal space: vulnerability. You have to be vulnerable to ask for help, to look deep inside and harness the power of liminal space. When it came to being vulnerable and accepting help from others, Dr. Kim didn't seem to have a choice. He had lost control of the left side of his body. When Rick saw him after his stroke, he was moving with a cane. But all of us could probably come up with examples of friends or colleagues who didn't show the same vulnerability when faced with such an overwhelming challenge.

> **You have to be vulnerable to ask for help, to look deep inside and harness the power of liminal space.**

Withdrawing into oneself is a far more typical response, particularly for the highly successful people we work with every day. They tend to have very deterministic views of the world, believing that if you want something in life, you should go get it—and do so on your own. Being faced with adversity can exacerbate that mindset. When you believe you should be able to seek out and achieve whatever you're looking to accomplish, it's hard to let other people help you move through it. But that's such a crucial piece of the puzzle. telos was fortunate to be a mechanism of support, to be there at a time when Dr. Kim needed us. But Dr. Kim made the deliberate choice to lean on those around him, and that was a catalytic component of his progress.

The willingness to accept support and to be vulnerable has become a superpower for Dr. Kim. He understands now that telling the stories of his scars is what brings people closer to him. It's what allows him to address and work his way through issues that arise at the most senior level of his organization. He doesn't arrive at the conference-room table in expert mode, as an untouchable force dictating next steps. Instead, he simply shares what he's experienced, saying, "Hey, my last team ran some bad plays when we were on the forty-yard line like we are today. Let me tell you what we learned."

And when he takes the lead on being vulnerable, he not only demonstrates to others that being vulnerable is okay but also invites *them* to be vulnerable, encouraging their development. His vulnerability has flywheel properties, creating immeasurable growth throughout the organization.

Empty Your Cup

There is a famous proverb that tells the story of a wise Zen master known for showing people the way to enlightenment. One day, a scholar arrived and asked the master to teach him what he knew. But it soon became evident that the scholar was more interested in sharing his own opinions than listening to the master's teachings.

"Why don't we have a cup of tea," the master suggested.

"Good idea," the scholar replied. The master handed the scholar a cup and began pouring. When the cup was halfway full, he kept pouring. He poured until the cup overflowed, tea spilling everywhere—on the table, on the floor, and onto the scholar himself.

"Stop!" the scholar shouted. "Can't you see that the cup is already full?"

The Zen master nodded. "You are like this cup. You have so many ideas that there is not room for anything else. Come back with an empty cup."[6]

---

6   Melissa Chu, "Empty Your Cup: A Zen Proverb on Accepting Feedback," Mission.org, October 11, 2017, https://medium.com/the-mission/empty-your-cup-a-zen-proverb-on-accepting-feedback-f1cce7bfe4a7.

In many ways, imposed periods of liminality—events that are not under your control, like the loss of a job, an illness, or the death of a loved one—compel the emptying of one's cup. Dr. Kim had to relearn so many fundamental things, including how to walk again. And in the process, he had to throw out everything he knew about his physical and professional life. He had to reevaluate what he had thought the future would look like. And with that challenge came unexpected benefits: a more fulfilling existence than he could have imagined previously.

Creating a Beginner's Mindset

Of course, you don't have to have a stroke to empty your cup and benefit from all the new learning doing so brings. You can make the decision to change your approach. Mark Benioff, founder, chairman, and co-CEO of Salesforce, a technology company valued at more than $135 billion, is committed to offering his employees the opportunity to clear their minds and approach challenges that present with a fresh perspective.[7] The majority of Salesforce's offices have "mindfulness zones" on every floor—clean, quiet spaces with mats and meditation cushions. The idea is that employees can unplug for a moment, placing their phones in a basket at the door, and use the silence to tap into new ideas. "Innovation is a core value at Salesforce," Benioff said. "It is deeply embedded in our culture. This starts in the mindset of every person in the company—you must cultivate a beginner's mind … A beginner's mind is the practice of looking at the world with fresh,

---

7   Catherine Clifford, "Salesforce CEO Marc Benioff: Why We have 'Mindfulness Zones' Where Employees Put Away Phones, Clear Their Minds," CNBC Make It, November 5, 2019, https://www.cnbc.com/2019/11/05/salesforce-ceo-marc-benioff-why-we-have-mindfulness-zones.html.

unencumbered eyes and avoiding inside-out or homogenous thinking that can lead to blind spots or missed opportunities."

The concept originates in Zen Buddhism, which instructs practitioners to maintain an open mind and avoid judgment, no matter how familiar a particular subject becomes. You can imagine how powerful adopting this mindset can be within the context of liminal space, and a quote from Benioff about his own reliance on the beginner's mindset reflects that: "Having a beginner's mind informs my management style. I'm trying to listen deeply, and the beginner's mind is informing me to step back, so that I can create what wants to be, not what was. I know that the future does not equal the past. I know that I have to be here in the moment." That kind of presence is key to navigating periods of uncertainty for yourself and making the best possible decisions for your team as well. We'll see that in the next chapter, as we meet a therapist tasked with taking the reins of an entire behavioral-health organization—and turning it around.

CHAPTER 4

the power of purpose.

How Liminality Presents for Teams

Vicki Clark was COO of Ravenwood Health, a nonprofit mental-health and addiction services organization. She had spent nearly thirty years there, and she was content to finish out her career in a role she found both fulfilling and comfortable. But one fateful day, she found out that the money issues the CEO had mentioned on occasion were actually much greater than he had let on; the organization was teetering on the edge of financial viability. That's when, on short notice, he retired—and called on Vicki to take over.

I had worked at Ravenwood Health for twenty-six years and spent most of them as COO, overseeing the clinical program. At the time, I knew that things were tight financially. Every so often, the CEO would tell me to pull back on spending, and I would do that. But I had no idea just how bad they were.

One day the CEO called me into his office. He closed the door and let me know that we had been running $10,000 short every month. I was stunned. But that news paled in comparison to what he said next. He told me he was retiring and that he was going to recommend that I take over as CEO. I was fifty-six years old at the time, and I had been COO for twenty-three years. I was pretty comfortable in my role, and I thought I would just finish things out there.

But I also knew something else: I didn't want to work for another person. I had always been ambitious, and I knew the agency inside and out—something that could work to my advantage. I was also incredibly passionate about my work; I have been blessed to be in a field I believe is right for me. So, I decided I would take on the challenge.

The board was a little reluctant to grant me the opportunity. They had always seen me as a quiet person, someone who only jumped in to support the CEO when necessary. They didn't really view me as a go-getter. I had to talk them into giving me a chance.

Once I did, I found out that things were more than a little tight. We were a $6 million agency with $500,000 in debt. We had totally maxed out our line of credit. Our billing department was almost nonexistent—just three billers, an accountant, and a supervisor. If they received a rejection from an insurance company, they would just throw it in a box, rather than correcting it and sending it back out the door. To put it mildly, things were not good.

And while I understood the financial piece of the organization's operations to some extent, I'd never gotten into the nitty-gritty—it just wasn't my area of expertise. For me, it was obvious that I needed to pull in people who had a good head for detail. But showing vulnerability, and sharing with my team that I didn't always know what I was doing, was a particular challenge for me.

In the past, I'd always taken everything upon myself. I had to learn how to sit back and let others help the organization flourish. I also had to show people that none of us had to be perfect, so they could feel like they could mess up too.

Once I let down my guard, I was able to rely on one of our clinicians who had gotten an accounting credential, and she helped me assess the billing department. We started pulling things apart and putting them back together, piece by piece. We had to bill for everything we could to begin closing the gap.

Meanwhile, we needed to take immediate action to cover ongoing expenses. I had a great relationship with our funders, and I reached out to the local mental-health and recovery board for help. They were willing to provide support temporarily, but it was still touch and go for a while. For months, we questioned whether we'd make payroll every single pay period.

In the midst of all of this, the CFO position was in flux. Our CFO left, and we hired someone new who went back to his organization after just eight months. Eventually, we found someone who helped us pull things together, but it would take a full two years to feel like we were steady financially.

As if that weren't enough, the state was making major changes to its behavioral-health protocol, which affected the programming we could offer, as well as our billing policies. A diagnosis for depression went from five billing codes to twenty-three billing codes. Rather than billing Medicaid expenses to the state, as we had in the past, we now had to bill them to five different agencies. I felt as if I were running on two different tracks: getting us in good financial shape and making sure that we were being proactive about the changes at the state level.

The next step was to ensure we were supporting our employees. We brought the telos institute on to provide our leadership team with coaching. One of the biggest transitions in terms of how we function came about thanks to our coaching experience. We learned to appreciate and understand different styles—the fact that, for instance, someone who is quieter and asks a lot of questions rather than jumping into a new task isn't necessarily resisting—they're processing. If you allow them to do that, they will be able to contribute more effectively. Coaching also brought out everyone's ability to be supportive of one another. Rather than functioning in our own little bubbles, we learned to ask how others were doing and how we could help.

As part of our coaching experience, some members of our team also shared that they dreamed about doing something professionally that differed from their current role. At first, we worried that they would end up chasing a dream that wasn't about us. Through coaching, though, we realized that it didn't benefit us to keep people from chasing their dreams—that it would only make them disgruntled about working with us. When we let go of that fear, we were also able to find ways to have people pursue their dreams here. One therapist was interested in pet therapy, and we paid for her to get certified. Now, she's bringing that passion to the agency, and everyone is excited about and benefiting from her new pursuit. Another person determined that they'd rather provide direct service than remain in a leadership position, and they are thriving in their new role, showing up with a different energy than they had previously.

We were also able to tap into the sense of purpose that is inherent in our field and to create a joint vision and establish our values—clearly delineating who we are and what we do. That enabled us to continue moving forward.

Going into the role of CEO, I had been intimidated by all that I didn't know—how to navigate liability insurance, personnel, and so on. But eventually, I embraced the fact that there were people out there who did know how to handle those things and that I could rely on them. At the beginning, I called our lawyer a lot and encouraged others to reach out to him when they had a question. I brought in consultants, allowing them to direct us. I also developed new skill sets. I became more purposeful about developing relationships and nurturing existing ones. I became more direct than I had been in the past. Today, I speak up without thinking twice about it—something I would have been very intimidated to do before this experience. I learned when to listen to other's opinions and when to make quick decisions.

And I saw similar changes in my team—dominant personalities who learned to step back and ask for opinions and introverted, internal processors who learned how to speak up and find ways to be heard—all while accepting who they are.

In the end, we were able to institute the necessary changes and come out on top. This year, we will bring in well over $9 million in revenue. And as a result of all this work, people are seeing and feeling the impact of our efforts. The agency has become an entirely different place to work. Employees are happy to be here. It has been exciting to watch, and I'm proud of what we've accomplished.

We remember the day of the leadership switch. Ravenwood's senior leadership team had called a meeting. It was a cold, rainy fall morning—a Saturday. None of us were quite sure what was happening; even key board members weren't sure where things were headed. Whether the agency would fold entirely was on the table. It was at that meeting that the CEO tendered his resignation and announced that Vicki would be his successor.

It was certainly a liminal point—for Vicki but also for her team. She would be leading a group that she was once a part of, and that reality would have an impact on everyone involved. Moreover, because Vicki wasn't familiar with the financial aspect of running an organization, she would have to rely on others to get the organization back on track. While her instinct may have been to portray that she had it all figured out, she just couldn't do that.

Dr. Brené Brown, research professor at University of Houston Graduate College of Social Work, speaker, and author of *Daring Greatly: How the Courage to Be Vulnerable Transforms the Way We Live, Love, Parent, and Lead,* has studied vulnerability, courage, worthiness, and shame for more than a decade.[8]

In her book, she explains that perfectionism is not the key to success. Rather, daring greatly—having the courage to show up and be seen—has far more potential in terms of your progress than attempting to maintain a flawless visage.

She notes, "Vulnerability is not knowing victory or defeat, it's understanding the necessity of both; it's engaging. It's being all in." And that's exactly what Vicki did. Her willingness to be vulnerable and let her team know what she needed helped them navigate their way out of some very deep water.

Vicki also acknowledged what others were feeling. When a longtime leader leaves, there are often a variety of responses from the team. Some people may find the change to be refreshing, while others may feel panic, worrying that their own jobs are on the line. Other members may be feeling angst or anger. And if the new leader is questioning her ability to take on this new responsibility, the team is likely questioning it too.

A common purpose that allows a team to bond is vital to moving in the same direction through liminal space.

---

8   Dan Schwabel, "Brene Brown: How Vulnerability Can Make Our Lives Better,"
     Forbes, April 21, 2013, https://www.forbes.com/sites/danschawbel/2013/04/21/
     brene-brown-how-vulnerability-can-make-our-lives-better/?sh=1033270636c7.

But if the team can find a common purpose—which, in Ravenwood Health's case, was their devotion to serving their patients—they can use that to make it to the other side. At Ravenwood, the cause became the galvanizing mechanism that allowed them to come together and hang on through those tough times. It allowed them to weather the rough seas as a unit until the tide could turn. A common purpose that allows a team to bond is vital to moving in the same direction through liminal space.

The Tuckman Model

Of course, it takes more than purpose to get on the same page, and it can help to understand the typical stages teams go through when forming or readjusting after a change in leadership. For insight, we can turn to the late Bruce Tuckman, a renowned organizational behaviorist. In 1965, he published a team development model that remains highly relevant today. It consists of four stages: forming, storming, norming, and performing.

Forming: At the beginning, teams are highly dependent on the leader for insight and guidance about where to go. The roles individuals will play and the responsibilities they'll take on aren't yet clear. Trust isn't there yet, leading members of the team to test the knowledge and abilities of the system and its leader. [9]

Storming: During the next stage, team members struggle as they work to find their position within the group. They may challenge each other and the leader. However, while those uncertainties remain, the purpose is becoming clearer. And that's good, because it is purpose that will help the team persist and progress toward a common goal.

---

9   "Tuckman: Forming, Storming, Norming, Performing model,"
     Businessballs, https://www.businessballs.com/team-management/
     tuckman-forming-storming-norming-performing-model/

Norming: In stage three, the team finds consensus. Roles and responsibilities are clearly defined, and agreement is reached more easily. Members also begin to understand their individual and collective working styles. They have built a framework of respect for the leader and for each other, and as a result of this progress, everyone is better equipped to take ownership of specific tasks.

Performing: In stage four, the team has hit its stride. The leader can step back and let the team operate, making collective decisions based on established criteria. Members can resolve any conflicts that arise among themselves and make appropriate changes to systems and processes as necessary. While the leader still delegates tasks and projects, the team doesn't need help accomplishing them.

Adjourning: In the 1970s, Tuckman added a fifth stage. This is just what it sounds like. At some point, the team completes its tasks and members move on. The goal here is to recognize when the end has arrived, the discomfort it may bring, and the opportunity to move on to new challenges.

Recognizing when the time to adjourn has come can be very difficult. Many of us are trained to keep the trains moving on time, but we haven't learned when it's time to stop—or how to effectively facilitate an ending.

Further, it's debatable as to whether adjourning is the last stage or the first, in that the way things end predicts how a new era will begin. That makes this stage extremely important, as—regardless of whether it marks the end or beginning—individuals and teams alike can take advantage of the circumstances at hand if they know what to look for. Often, it's adjourning—the end of a particular event, experience, or relationship—that launches one into liminal space. For Vicki and the entire Ravenwood team, the financial problems that were no longer sustainable for the organization and the CEO's departure served as the opportunity to establish a new beginning.

The same proved to be true for another client of ours, a hospital system working to evaluate its palliative-care program. The administration had seen the program strictly as a way to manage endings, as families experienced the program at the end of a patient's life. But we recognized that a family's encounter with the palliative-care program could actually mark the beginning of their relationship with the institution.

If they had a positive experience with the staff and facility during one of the most difficult times in their lives, they were more likely to return when expecting a baby, seeking pediatric care for their children, or needing treatment for an emergency, like a broken bone. When the hospital system recognized that the palliative-care program could be an entry point for patients, they were able to harness the opportunity to cultivate new relationships—to the benefit of the institution as a whole and those it served.

When Successful Plays Stop Delivering

At the beginning of the journey for Vicki and the team at Ravenwood Health, the organization was experiencing a key marker of liminal space: the same plays they had been running for years weren't working anymore, and they weren't sure why. Things just didn't feel right.

Back in late 2008, when the financial markets were imploding and Lehman Brothers was going out of business, many companies—and their leaders—were in a similar position. During that tumultuous period, Rick found himself on the top floor of a Manhattan office tower playing a very small role in a meeting of senior leaders at UBS Financial Services. One of the leaders was the CEO of US Wealth

Management, Marten Hoekstra. Binders were flying. The McKinsey consultants were in the room. Rick hadn't planned to speak up, but for some reason he was compelled to do so. He addressed the CEO from the other end of the table, his voice rising above the cacophony. "Marten," he said. "What are we really trying to accomplish here?"

The CEO looked left, he looked right, and then he said, simply, "I don't know." Rick had had significant respect for him before that moment, but right then, it escalated considerably. And he wasn't the only one who felt that way. Marten's vulnerability and his willingness to be honest galvanized the team in the room and generated a degree of clarity that did not exist prior to his answer.

The moment was also significant for telos, as it ratified our name. *Telos* is a Greek word first used by Aristotle to mean "with the end in mind." Liberating the energy necessary for clients to reach their aspired destinations requires, first and foremost, understanding what and where those destinations actually are. But that clarity, even for the leader of a global Fortune 50 company, can be elusive. At any point in time, one can lose their way. If it could happen to Marten Hoekstra, it can happen to any of us. And admitting what you don't know to your team can have powerful results. It can serve to help you identify the new plays necessary for the next era. You can then ask important questions like, *What was working before? What's worth taking with us? What do we want to change? How do we do that?* to figure out where to head next.

Today, Ravenwood has purchased a new building, and they're seeing the shift in physical space as a new period of liminality. We've worked with them to process this change, asking questions to help them determine what they want to bring with them into this new facility and era of their organization.

Together, we have created a piece of art that roots them in their past successes while propelling them forward. Each member of the team was given a piece of fabric. On it, they wrote a word or phrase that captured either something they wanted to bring with them or something they wanted to accomplish moving forward. All those pieces of fabric were sewn together to create a collage. It will have a home in the lobby of the new facility and thus serve as a front-and-center reminder of where they came from and where they're going.

Put the Pedal to the Metal

Remember *Days of Thunder*? It's essentially *Top Gun* on wheels. Tom Cruise stars as Cole Trickle, a young NASCAR driver. After a bad accident, he has trouble getting back on the track; he's reluctant to give it his all. His pit-crew chief, Harry Hogge, played by Robert Duvall, tells Trickle that when he sees a crash ahead of him, he should put the pedal to the metal and drive right at it, because by the time he gets there, the crash will have dispersed. He'll be able to speed on through. Meanwhile, what does everyone else do? They take their foot off the pedal. As such, pushing forward provides a significant advantage.

Navigating a liminal period works similarly—you must drive forward. That way, once the smoke has cleared and everyone catches up to what's happening, you'll be out in front. If you are practiced, prepared, and principled, you can keep moving; and the ground you'll cover in the midst of that liminal period can make all the difference in the world.

But it's also a heck of a lot easier to point the steering wheel straight and go all out on the straightaways. The challenge comes on the curves. That's where the race is won and lost and where our abilities as leaders to manage these points of liminality serve as the ultimate difference maker, particularly in business today—an environment that has never been more volatile, uncertain, complex, and ambiguous. And while you might assume that confidence or determination is what dictates a leader's success, that's only half the equation.

A Winning Formula: Confidence and Humility

Successfully leading a team requires both confidence and humility. Making it to the other side requires strength combined with an honesty about our shortcomings, or lack of knowledge or experience. The combination allows us to move through. Dr. Kim and Vicki Clark each demonstrated both qualities. Vicki first believed that she had to have it all figured out, but acknowledging what she didn't know and calling on others to provide the help she needed, while demonstrating confidence in what she *did* know, helped her shepherd her team to a better place.

At telos, we often work to coax this combination from leaders, asking, "Are you confident enough to believe that you can be great? Are you humble enough to know you can't do it on your own?" Many leaders are a bit confused by these questions. *Wait, I thought I was great already. That's how I became head of this place*, they may think. But this is about transcendence, and that requires an acknowledgment that there is farther to go and that getting there will take confidence and humility in equal measure. If they can acknowledge there is more ground to cover and that they can't do it alone, they have the potential to do something really special.

Can You Trust Your Team with Your Weakness?

But finding that balance doesn't come easily. It's hard to trust each other enough to be vulnerable in one another's presence. It's hard for leaders to say, "I don't know how to do that. Can you help me?" They worry that showing vulnerability will make them lesser, but it doesn't. We have to be able to trust each other with our weakness. It's a crucial foundation on which to build everything else.

Author and business management expert Patrick Lencioni coined the term *vulnerability-based trust* to describe a crucial element of successful teams. It differs greatly from what he refers to as "predictive trust," the concept that teams come to trust each other because they've worked together for a long time and can therefore predict what other members are going to do—regardless of what they say. Meanwhile, with vulnerability-based trust, people are comfortable enough to be honest about how they feel and what they can and can't do. They "can and will genuinely say things to one another like 'I don't know the answer,' 'I need help,' 'I made a mistake.'" They trust each other inherently. But, he explains, the only way to achieve that is "if the leader goes first. People have to know that the leader is going to take that leap of faith and be vulnerable, and that is going to give [the team] permission to do so also."[10] As the leader, it's up to you to set the standard.

Lead with Empathy

Another key part of effectively driving change for your team is leading with empathy. There is a difference between empathy and sympathy.

---

10   Patrick Lencioni, "Vulnerability-Based Trust," YouTube, May 16, 2017, https://www.youtube.com/watch?v=mFC-AqO9V80.

Sympathy refers to feelings of pity or sorrow for someone else's situation; you feel for them, but very much from the perspective of an outsider. On the other hand, empathy involves putting oneself in someone else's shoes to clearly imagine what they're going through.

Brené Brown describes empathy as "feeling with people." In a short video, she further teases out the distinction. "Empathy is this sacred space where someone is in this deep hole and they shout out from the bottom, 'I'm stuck; it's dark; I'm overwhelmed.' And then we look, and we say, 'Hey, I know what it's like down here, and you're not alone.' Sympathy is 'Oo, it's bad, uh huh. No. You want a sandwich?'"

As you might guess, it's much more challenging to be empathetic. As Brown explains, "Empathy is a choice, and it's a vulnerable choice because in order to connect with you, I have to connect with something in myself that knows that feeling."[11] But making that choice will make all the difference.

Tapping into Tribe Mentality

Now that she's on the other side, Vicki knows—first and foremost—that the primary impetus or impediment to a team's success is the leader, closely followed by the team. Hers was able to maintain their purpose and find their way amid a lot of uncertainty. What they knew for sure throughout was that their work was important, and that kept them connected and making progress. With a common goal and a trustworthy leader, they became a tribe. But that tribe mentality also extends to people *outside* your organization or team, those who can help you get a clear perspective or support you through liminal space.

---

11   Brené Brown, "Brené Brown on Empathy," YouTube, December 10, 2013, https://www.youtube.com/watch?v=1Evwgu369Jw.

Picture a local community pool. There's the central pool with its lap lanes, the shallow play area, and a whirlpool. Now, focus in on the whirlpool, and imagine a beach ball right in the center, caught up in the vortex of spinning water. The beach ball continues to spin in that vortex. There's an exit, of course, but 270 degrees of that whirlpool are closed, and the whirlpool's walls keep the beach ball contained and moving around and around continuously, so that it's hard to exit. Being in liminal space is like being that beach ball in the swirl of the whirlpool. Getting out requires some sort of disruption, the additional energy necessary to force the ball out of the spin and to the edge of the pool. Otherwise, it will stay in there indefinitely.

More often than not, making it to the edge requires the support of others—someone with a fresh perspective or vantage point—a person on the edge of that whirlpool who can help pull that beach ball out of the water.

Gianpiero Petriglieri, a medical doctor and associate professor of organizational behavior at INSEAD, describes the power of building a tribe: a tightknit community that "[keeps] our working lives exciting and us stable, ultimately helping us master [them]." He found that even those who claimed to thrive working on their own still needed a tribe to be successful. "Without them," he explained, "those same lives might make us bored or too anxious."[12] A tribe is all the more important when you know you're in liminal space. In liminal periods, think about what you need from others. Ask yourself who you can reach out to and what you can ask of them.

On the flip side, think about how you can best support others when you recognize that they are in liminal space. These are times when others need us most—and also when we tend to look in the

---

12　Gianpiero Petriglieri, "To Take Charge of Your Career, Start by Building Your Tribe," Harvard Business Review, April 5, 2018, https://hbr.org/2018/04/to-take-charge-of-your-career-start-by-building-your-tribe.

other direction. We often associate a certain contagiousness with those going through big life changes—believing that if we get too close, maybe we'll wind up in a similar situation. But logically, we can recognize that's not the case and instead concentrate on the fact that liminal spaces are all around us, precious, tender, and bursting with potential. If we can better recognize them and support others experiencing them, we'll all be better off.

Of course, team experiences aren't just bound to the office; they're all around us, occurring in our personal lives too. Families function as their own teams, and they, too, experience liminal space as their circumstances change. For example, when a child goes off to college, it often creates a period of disruption or liminality not just for the child but also for the family at large. While the child is grappling with that in-between space, where they don't quite live on their own yet, but they don't live at home anymore, everyone is navigating the environment that transition creates. *What does the team look like after their departure? How do you stay engaged when one member of the team is essentially working remotely? And how does that person fit back into the family when they're home on vacation?* If you can look to the tenets covered in this chapter, remembering that sense of purpose, leading with empathy, cultivating vulnerability-based trust, and more, you can find your way to a different—and often better—reality.

CHAPTER 5

maintaining perspective and purpose through change.

How Liminality Presents for Organizations

You're probably familiar with the J.M. Smucker Company, more colloquially—and affectionately—known as Smucker's. Their signature jams and jellies may have graced your childhood pantry or that of your grandparents; after all, the company has been around for more than 120 years.

Today, the range of products and brands under the Smucker umbrella is far broader than ever before. As a result, 90 percent of American homes are stocked with at least one Smucker product.[13] You may be serving Smucker's to your children, your grandchildren, even your pets whether you know it or not. But the J.M. Smucker Company's work to stand—and expand—their ground in an ever-evolving marketplace hasn't been easy, particularly as they grappled with two different

---

13   "From Our Family to Yours," J.M. Smucker Company, https://www.jmsmucker.com/about.

yet concurrent liminal elements: a change in leadership and a rapidly evolving industry.

In May of 2016, Mark T. Smucker took over as president and chief executive officer of Smucker, becoming the fifth generation to lead the company. For Mark, who had grown up personally and professionally within the Smucker organization, the transition provided a lot of, well, food for thought.

At the same time, the packaged food industry—of which the J.M. Smucker Company had always been a part—was undergoing a transformation. The same businesses and branding strategies that had always been growth drivers for them just weren't realizing the same kind of gains. While Smucker had long had the market cornered on the center aisles of the grocery store—the area dominated by packaged and nonperishable foods—things began to change. Consumers were starting to prioritize the ease and convenience of online purchasing, choosing brands based on price and availability rather than recognition, and turning the Smucker's economic model upside down in the process.

Other changes were also afoot. While families across America had historically turned to packaged foods to make daily meal preparation and celebrations alike easier, an increased interest in natural and organic grocery items was having a negative impact on the sales of products like Pillsbury boxed cakes and frostings, a company Smucker had purchased prior to the boom in healthier foods.[14] The company had yet to reflect this reality or other societal shifts that had occurred in the past several years in its products or advertising. For example, Smucker's Jif peanut butter had had a variation of the same tagline, "Choosy moms choose Jif," for decades. But in the 2010s, dads were

---

14   Erica Kincaid, "Smucker Sells Pillsbury, Other U.S. Baking Brands for $375M," FoodDive, July 10, 2018, https://www.fooddive.com/news/smucker-is-considering-a-sale-of-its-baking-brands-for-700m/518793/.

likely to be making those grocery runs too. What about them? And what about families with two dads? Or those headed by grandparents or other relatives?

Leaders from the companies Smucker had acquired began to sound the alarms, warning that change was coming for the industry. They pointed out that Smucker might want to reconsider their approach in a number of areas.

But when those changes and warnings first began arising, they were almost invisible to the J.M. Smucker Company and its leadership, because no one was looking for them. Things had been going according to plan for over a century, since J.M. Smucker himself established the company. Few at the company expected the impact of the disruption, and it was challenging for them to recognize evidence that the disruption was already beginning.

However, eventually, the reality of the situation became clear. This Fortune 500 company, headquartered in the sleepy, traditional town of Orrville, Ohio—where its founder first began selling cider and apple butter from the back of his horse-drawn wagon more than a century ago—had to make some changes to keep up. A longtime client of telos, president and CEO Mark Smucker, shared insight into his transition and that of the company:

I was tremendously excited to have the opportunity to be the next family steward of the company. The brands and the people are what get me out of bed and into work every day; they're the aspects of the company that I'm most passionate about. I knew I had the opportunity to make the changes necessary to usher the company into the next few decades. I knew I had a chance to make sure the organization could rise to meet the changes, challenges, and opportunities present in the marketplace, while making the world a better place along the way. It was a privilege to have the chance to make that kind of impact.

But the weight of the responsibility was not lost on me. To make a significant impact, I had to make sure we preserved and grew our brands and our people. I knew we had to make sure that we kept our finger on the pulse of not only what was happening outside the company but also what was happening inside it. I knew that would require a greater degree of transparency, including a much more frequent cadence of communication and the implementation of tools to gather feedback from the organization at large—from surveys to focus groups.

As I thought about all the changes I was excited to make, I also knew I needed a great team that was capable of helping to drive those changes. I surrounded myself with people who are smarter than me, people with different points of view. Doing so helped me—and us as a team— try to make the right decisions.

But cultivating a strong team would require some changes as well. In November 2019, with telos's support, the company instituted a new executive leadership structure to "sharpen the company's focus on strategic initiatives, enhance accountability for business delivery, streamline decision-making, and enable greater agility to ensure delivery of strategic and financial priorities."

Among the staffing changes, Geoff Tanner, who had previously been senior vice president of growth and consumer engagement, was elected chief marketing and commercial officer and tasked with leading marketing, innovation, insights, and e-commerce, as well as US retail sales and market development. Amy Held, who had been senior vice president of corporate strategy, M&A, and international, was elected chief strategy and international officer and would continue to lead corporate strategy, M&A, and international functions. Both would report to Mark Smucker directly.[15] Together, they would pave a new way forward through the rough terrain of liminal space.

In early 2020, Mark, Amy, and Geoff shared their takes on what had unfolded as they entered liminal space. And one of the first challenges they encountered was recognizing that they were in it.

"There were a few moments when we felt acutely that we were at a key inflection point, that the plays we ran yesterday weren't working any longer," Mark said. For example, when Smucker began integrating Big Heart Pet Brands, a leading pet food company it acquired in 2015, Mark felt the challenge of navigating uncharted territory and building capabilities that the company hadn't quite developed. But overall, it was difficult to pinpoint a single seminal moment that marked their entrance into liminal space.

"The plays don't suddenly not work; they just become less effective over time for different people at different points of that journey," Geoff said. "I would say the way we used to do marketing didn't suddenly die; it had been slip-sliding away for three to four years."

"Or a decade," Mark said.

Geoff and Amy both noted that having a specific moment at which to point may have actually made it easier to drive change throughout the organization. "I wish we could have created a truly

---

15   "The J.M. Smucker Company Announces Evolution of Executive Leadership Structure and Team," Cision, November 13, 2019, https://www.prnewswire.com/news-releases/the-j-m-smucker-company-announces-evolution-of-executive-leadership-structure-and-team-300957861.html.

burning platform, because without that, I think people felt they had a bit of a choice [in terms of embracing change]," Geoff said.

That meant that once Mark took over, he would have his work cut out for him. Amy offered insight into the transition. "Mark was taking over as CEO at a time of unbelievable disruption in our industry. We had just announced a massive acquisition that had had a huge impact on us as a company. Because both inflection points were happening simultaneously, he couldn't just keep the plane flying straight."

"He had to help the organization navigate that industry change at the right pace in the midst of his own shift. There was the pressure to do things differently, to drive better results, and he had to know when to sacrifice speed or change based on where members of the organization were at. He had to balance how quickly we would adapt to the market with where the organization was and determine how best to do that. There were moments where he leaned in and said 'burn the ships,' like when he made the decision to transform our marketing model. And there were other times when he had the savvy to know that we'd have to move at a slower pace."

"Mark has a view and mindset that says, 'What we do within our four walls is one thing, but we need to be just as tuned in—or more so—to what's happening outside them.' That helps us calibrate things. If you're just focusing on what you're doing and the changes you want to make, you may miss some of the key learning opportunities along the way. And that's critical at this point in time."

Geoff echoed Amy's observations: "I would say the challenges to our industry status reared their heads within a month of when Mark took the helm. Ninety-nine percent of people didn't see it. But he had a very strong stance on what was happening externally and thus what had to happen internally. He managed the degree of change he was driving in the organization, measuring it against two elements: how much was actually needed given what was occurring in the outside world, and how much he felt we could push internally."

"Mark is also a systemic thinker," Amy said. "He's able to see the different moving pieces and respect that each one must be looked at. I think that approach is what enables him to make better, more balanced choices. He is able to put an individual situation in the context of the broader goals."

One of the areas that required the careful calibration of internal change with external demand was the amount of digital transformation required for Smucker to be successful. To that end, Geoff said, "If you pick up any industry publication or speak with a consultant, they'll tell you that you need more digital, digital, digital. But we have been moderating that feedback in terms of what is truly valuable to our organization. There are a lot of false promises in that space and others.

"I think some of the best decisions we've made as a company have been those we didn't make. For example, a few years ago, there was a lot of pressure to get into the direct-to-consumer business, that we should be making a deal with plated.com or Blue Apron. We didn't. Meanwhile, the decision to do so ended up causing real issues for many of our competitors.

"On the other hand, we knew we had to engage in some of what we were seeing externally. The new creative Smucker has put out is a great example." Days after we spoke with the Smucker team, Jif launched a digital marketing campaign in collaboration with GIF-sharing site Giphy, on how to pronounce both the peanut butter brand, with a soft *g*, and the bite-size video clips—with a hard *g*. The collaboration included Jif GIFs, a hashtag (#JifvsGif), as well as limited-edition "Giphy x Jif Jars," that sold out within hours of the campaign's launch.[16]

"We wrestled with how to do it but ultimately determined to lean in, and I think it was the right call," Geoff added.

Eventually, all three executives agreed that they would have to continue to read the external environment and make decisions about how to adapt. "We all know that we have to continue the journey of change and transformation," Mark said. "Let's face it, there is probably no end to this journey, but there is a moment where our continued evolution should become natural."

"You know," Amy chimed in, "one of the best things you did, Mark, was surround yourself most closely with an executive leadership team of people who are anchored in different areas of the organization. There are some people who have been here for a very long time and have perspective on where we've been, what has made us successful, and how we have stayed and can stay true to who we are. And at the same time, there are others who haven't been here for many years and provide a different perspective. Thinking about it from different angles helps to make sense of it all."

We maintain our commitment to each other through constant communication.

Geoff also noted the importance of effectively cultivating an openness to change across an organization during liminal periods: "It's also about fostering that open dialogue, where you don't need to have the right answer—because no one does. When I think about where Mark has helped us be successful, it's in fostering those kinds of conversations

---

16   Robert Williams, "Jif seeks to settle the debate about 'GIF' Pronunciation," Mobile Marketer, February 26, 2020, https://www.mobilemarketer.com/news/jif-seeks-to-settle-the-debate-about-gif-pronunciation/572978/.

where we can roll around in it without having the right answer and just have the opportunity to debate and discuss."

Mark agreed, adding, "We maintain our commitment to each other through constant communication—it's one of the capabilities we have to embrace. Communicating information at the right time can bring the organization along. And though we may disagree, at the end of the day, once we arrive at a decision—however we get there—everyone must lock arms and walk out of the room ready to help drive that decision forward."

Of course, ushering in widespread transformation came with its own set of growing pains—including staffing changes. Geoff said, "Mark, I think you were hopeful, as we all were, that we would be able to adjust to what was going on around us with less change. But as you've gotten into it, you've seen—and adapted—to the reality. There were moments when you recognized that certain members of the team weren't going to make the journey with us. It may have felt harsh, but it sent a signal in terms of the leadership behaviors you wanted and those you didn't."

"It's interesting," Amy began, "I'm finding that when we've anchored our employees around our core values and then try to introduce change, we find ourselves with a lot of people who have their own view of why the way we do things now is reflective of our soul as a company and use that to justify keeping things the same. It can be a struggle to help people parse out that it's okay to change the way we think through and do things—that making those adjustments doesn't necessarily change who you are.

"How do you do that successfully? How do you get people to let go of stagnation and embrace change? You've got to create a bit of a safe space, telling them that at the end of all this, we will still be who we are. It doesn't necessarily mean that everything we're going to do is going to be the same as it is today, but that's okay. To get that point across, we often talk about our values," Amy said. "We call them our Basic Beliefs."

"One thing that we have always said is that we have to be willing to change everything about our business, even our strategy," Mark said. "But what should never change is our core values and our commitment to each other. That must remain the bedrock underlying how we make and implement decisions. We've been on this journey for a few years—if not longer. I'm proud to say that we have continued to conduct ourselves with the principles of mutual respect and resonant leadership. We've learned we have the intestinal fortitude to make really difficult decisions and to do it in a way that is respectful of our colleagues and the folks around us on a broader, more global scale. As a result, we have been able to preserve who we are at the core and our fundamental values as a company."

To succeed in a new consumer climate, the Smucker team had to make adjustments across almost every aspect of the business, a process that required extensive reflection, multiple perspectives, and some difficult decisions. How do you steer an organization through liminal space, particularly when you are facing disruption in multiple areas of your operation, as Smucker was? For insight, we can turn to the telos levers of organizational performance.

The telos Levers for Organizational Performance

When addressing liminal space from an organizational perspective, our goal is to improve overall performance by addressing the factors that have the greatest impact on success. To do this, we align what we have deemed the telos levers for organizational performance—

purpose, people, product, process, and performance—to not only meet pressing needs, but also achieve long-term prosperity.

Let's take a closer look at how each of these levers provides an opportunity to both evaluate and make an impact on our operations at large.

- **Purpose** quite simply refers to one's reason for being, and to truly be successful, *what* we do and *how* we do it must align with *why* we do it.

- Having the right **people**, in the right places, focused on the right outcomes, has a measurable impact on organizational performance.

- A review of **product** draws our attention to the choices we make about deliverables, whether tangible or intangible, and whether these meet or exceed market demands and customer expectations.

- The **process** by which we operate, sequence the creation of deliverables, and communicate internally provides a picture of predictability, stability, and organizational sustainability.

- What we track and measure gets done, which is why a thoughtful and deliberate approach to **performance** is so critical. A transformational performance indicator will not only identify the key metric(s) that signal current success but also act as a catalyst for organizational performance today and tomorrow.

Which of the levers is most important and thus most pressing? That depends. While alignment of all five levers is always the ultimate objective, to determine which of the levers will have the biggest impact on organizational performance in your operation, consider your customer's perspective. If customers are happy with price, but would like more (or fewer) features from your offerings, then it may be wise to address the **product** lever first. If your organization seems to have lost its soul amid the inevitable changes that occur over the course of a business's evolution, then consider starting with **purpose.** If your business requires better engagement or commitment from its **people,** then having well-trained and highly motivated team members is most important. If ensuring that your high-quality product reaches your customers' hands in an efficient and timely fashion is a key part of your strategy, then **process** may be your initial focus. And if your market conditions seem to be in a constant state of flux, perhaps you might tackle all five telos levers and keep them in a continuous performance improvement cycle. To help you delve deeper into each lever and uncover ways to optimize it, we have included some key questions to consider at the end of this chapter.

In the J.M. Smucker Company's case, four areas of the organization were in transition. People elements were changing. Not only had Mark taken over as president and CEO but the organization was also making significant changes to its leadership team as a whole.

They were making adjustments to their product lines, as well. Smucker had been a growth company for a long time, but in recent years, growth just wasn't happening at the same rate. The company had been acquiring new brands for years—including Jif peanut butter in 2002, Pillsbury in 2004, and Folgers in 2008—with positive results. Smucker also purchased a premium pet food company in 2015, when previously their sole focus had been on feeding people. While pet food was a far cry from peanut butter and jelly, it was a logical move given the US's rapidly changing food and beverage market; namely that pet food and snacks had come to lead center-of-the-store sales, with annual retail sales totaling $97 billion and projected to reach

$168 billion by 2029.[17], [18] Net sales grew 5 percent a year from 2011 to 2016, and cash flow expanded from $211 million to $1.3 billion during the same time period.

In 2017, the company expected a slowdown, anticipating a 1 percent decrease in sales as they planned to reduce prices on their coffee products, while profits increased. That year, sales dropped 7 percent, reflecting lower pet food sales in addition to that planned price decrease in their coffee segment, while coffee profits remained strong. The shift reflected the company's transition from brand acquirer to manager and corresponding efforts to streamline the business at large.[19]

Their product line would require some tinkering. With changing interests among its human consumers, the company decided to sell its US baking business—including household and once-household name brands like Pillsbury, Martha White, Hungry Jack, White Lily, and Jim Dandy—which had seen a significant drop in sales.[20]

Smucker continues to make progress, adjusting various areas to maintain and grow their position in the marketplace. As the team turns their attention to each of the telos levers, they find themselves navigating circumstances that are part and parcel of liminal space. For example, Mark, Amy, and Geoff mentioned a common obstacle when

17   Jennifer Semple, "Smucker to Acquire Maker of Rachael Ray Nutrish Pet Food," Food Business News, April 4, 2018, https://www.foodbusinessnews.net/articles/11596-smucker-to-acquire-maker-of-rachael-ray-nutrish-pet-food.

18   Rhian Hunt, "Is J.M. Smucker Barking Up the Wrong Tree by Focusing On Pet Foods?" The Motley Fool, February 28, 2020, https://www.fool.com/investing/2020/02/28/for-nathan-is-jm-smucker-barking-up-the-wrong-tree.aspx.

19   Nicholas Rossolillo, "J.M. Smucker: Transformational Growth Story or Stagnating Food Business?" The Motley Fool, September 8, 2016, https://www.fool.com/investing/2016/09/08/jm-smucker-transformational-growth-story-or-stagna.aspx.

20   Erica Kincaid, "Smucker Sells Pillsbury, Other U.S. Baking Brands for $375M," FoodDive, July 10, 2018, https://www.fooddive.com/news/smucker-is-considering-a-sale-of-its-baking-brands-for-700m/518793/.

it comes to the people lever: resistance to change. To better understand this phenomenon, we can turn to organizational psychologists Robert Kegan and Lisa Laskow Lahey and their concept of competing commitments.

Uncovering Competing Commitments

Why is resistance to change among employees so common, even when its necessity is so apparent? Kegan and Lahey's research "led [them] to a surprising yet deceptively simple conclusion. Resistance to change does not reflect opposition, nor is it merely a result of inertia. Instead, even as they hold a sincere commitment to change, many people are unwittingly applying productive energy toward a hidden *competing commitment*. The resulting dynamic equilibrium stalls the effort in what looks like resistance but is in fact a kind of personal immunity to change."[21]

Often, that competing commitment is hidden even from the employee herself. For example, someone may worry that if she successfully tackles a challenging assignment—even one she is passionate about—the next one that comes along will be altogether too difficult. As a result, she can't seem to get started. The good news is that when those competing commitments are brought to light, it is possible to overcome them—a relieving outcome for employers and employees alike, since immense frustration often accompanies that resistance to change. As Kegan and Lahey explain, "Employees are almost always tremendously relieved when they discover just *why* they feel as if they are rolling a boulder up a hill only to have it roll back down again."[22]

---

21 Robert Kegan and Lisa Laskow Lahey, "The Real Reason People Won't Change," Harvard Business Review, November 2001.

22 Kegan and Lahey, "The Real Reason People Won't Change."

The first step is to uncover competing commitments. How do you do that? Ask questions. Kegan and Lahey recommend beginning with, *What would you like to see changed at work, so that you could be more effective or so that work would be more satisfying?* This question almost always unearths a complaint, something managers often find frustrating. However, "people complain only about the things they care about, and they complain the loudest about the things they care about most."[23] As such, those complaints can easily be transformed into powerful commitments that spur, rather than stall, progress.

Once those commitments are revealed, employees are often able to understand the ways in which they have gotten in their own way. The next step is to mine for the worries or discomfort that accompany changing their behavior. If we return to our previous example, that employee's procrastination may be a preventive measure, helping her avoid failure if a more difficult task is doled out. As you can see, the competing commitment is really a form of self-protection. And it is tied to what Kegan and Lahey refer to as "*big assumptions*—deeply rooted beliefs [people have] about themselves and the world around them."

Of course, those assumptions are not necessarily accurate—not at all. Who is to say that our employee would fail if she were to take on a greater challenge? When employees can understand that, they can begin to challenge their big assumptions—and counter them.

Stay Rooted

As you begin thinking about the telos levers and their role in current and future success, it's important to note that some areas may not require significant adjustments, if any at all. The first step in success-

---

23 Kegan and Lahey, "The Real Reason People Won't Change."

fully executing change of any kind is acknowledging and cataloging the enduring components—the elements that will remain a part of the foundation even as we move forward.

Successful growth and expansion require a rootedness, a set of guiding principles, goals, and commitments to which the organization, its leadership, and employees at all levels can continue to hold fast, even when it seems everything else is up in the air. For Smucker, various aspects of the business continue to shift, but one element remains: their commitment to their purpose—one that doesn't stray far from what J.M. Smucker first envisioned all those years ago. The company's Basic Beliefs, a set of principles that have served as a guiding force since its inception, will continue to serve that purpose.

Smucker's Basic Beliefs:

- Quality
- People
- Ethics
- Growth
- Independence

The J.M. Smucker Company's Basic Beliefs are the foundation for future strategy, plans, and accomplishments.

They serve as guideposts for decision-making and daily interactions with consumers, customers, employees, suppliers, communities, and shareholders."[24] The beliefs focus on putting quality first; maintaining a fair environment for employees that prioritizes personal responsibility at work and beyond; upholding the company's long-standing ethical values of honesty, respect, trust, responsibility, and fairness; a forward-looking approach to growth; and preserving the company's independence and culture.

---

24 "Our Basic Beliefs," J.M. Smucker Company, https://www.jmsmucker.com/about/Values/our-basic-beliefs.

In a situation in which everything was in flux, those Basic Beliefs—the Smucker Company's foundation—endured. When it comes to your organization, what must change? What will endure?

As we move on to the second half of the book, we will continue to reflect on these concepts within the context of a somewhat different perspective and strategy. We've seen the ways in which people and organizations facing liminal space harnessed that disruptive period to achieve success that would have previously exceeded their imaginations. But what if we could create those kinds of disruptions, and the fertile ground they create, for ourselves? What if we could design our own path to transformation? Let's find out.

Before you move on to the next chapter, consider the telos levers as they relate to your organization. Ask yourself—and your leadership team—the following questions.

purpose

› What is our reason for being?
› What matters most to me, our team, our organization?
› Can our employees, customers, etc. identify our core values based on our behavior?
› Are we maintaining our purpose as we strive to meet our business objectives?
› If our organization didn't exist tomorrow, to whom would it matter and why?

people

› What uniquely identifies and binds the people in our organization?
› What are our team roles and associated responsibilities and goals?
› Have we clearly defined our target markets, key partners, suppliers, vendors, etc.?
› What unique skills and shared genius does our organization possess?
› Do we celebrate diversity and the unique greatness our colleagues possess?

product

› What are we truly in the business of providing?
› What challenges or opportunities do we help our customers overcome and leverage?
› Are we clear about what we offer and equally clear about what we don't?
› Do we have a definable, repeatable, scaleable and differentiating client experience?

process

› What is the rhythm and cadence by which our organization operates?
› How are decisions made?
› How does work flow from role to role?
› What are the mechanisms for collaboration?
› What are our high impact activities?
› How will we know when processes are working as best they can?
› What are our strategies to overcome hurdles?
› Who has power and authority over various operational steps?

performance

› What do we track and measure?
› What are our critical few objectives and associated metrics?
› Do our metrics align with our values and enable us to achieve our mission?
› Do our objectives align with our strengths and overall goals?
› How is our behavior shaped by individual, team, and organizational goals?
› How do we assess progress?
› What does it look like when we win?

CHAPTER 6

what if we could catalyze our own transformation?

Everything appears starker on the Boulder Mail Trail, a trek through Utah's ancient ruins, hidden gorges, canyon narrows, arches, and bridges. On the trail, which tracks the path mail and telegraph carriers took between the towns of Boulder and Escalante in the 1900s, the flowers are more vivid—colors so saturated you might think your fingers would sink into the petals as if they were wet paint. The night is darker than back home, the stars brighter.

It's so quiet, but when you stop to listen, you start to hear bird songs, the hum of insects, the creak and swish of wind through sagebrush and juniper.

In places like these, you can't help but grapple with millennia of geographic history and its uncanny ability to reflect your own impermanence. You feel the full weight of your existence and your utter insignificance—a speck against gargantuan walls of slickrock and unending open skies—all at once. This environment provides a unique opportunity: to leverage this very moment. To be transported out of space and time and into the crevices and winding routes of your own mind. To examine where you've been and consider where you might go.

This, too, is liminal space, brought on not by a sudden or unexpected event like the death of a loved one or a drop in the market—a reality thrust upon you—but of your own volition. It's what we call *curated liminality*, and it is the basis of our Leadership Ventures—the most immersive expression of the liminal experiences we provide and help clients unpack.

Leadership Ventures are yearlong development experiences that include 120-plus hours of interaction, including both group development and one-on-one coaching, and offer the opportunity to leave behind your typical surroundings and daily routines and immerse yourself in an unfamiliar environment for five to ten days. That departure from the day-to-day predisposes you to think differently, to examine yourself, your business strategies, and your key relationships from a perspective too often unattainable while staring at the same four walls of your office or the rooms of your home. It gives you the chance to dig deep into your consciousness, while testing the edges of your physical capabilities. The result? Transformative growth that sticks.

Why are these experiences so powerful? The lion's share of the time, even the most self-aware of us don't realize that we're entering periods of liminality, and therein lies the opportunity.

We believe that catalyzing our own transitions builds the muscle for navigating those we don't initiate. Author Bruce Feiler's work supports this concept. He conducted 225 in-depth interviews investigating how individuals handled one or more of fifty-two kinds of life transitions. He found that life is far less linear than many of us assume it will be. We no longer live in a world where we can bank on having one job, relationship, or source of happiness over the course of our existence. Through his research, he saw that those who anticipated and embraced the inevitable transitions that occur were most successful at managing them.[25]

The ability to craft and manage liminality strategically presents us with unbridled potential.

In some instances, we are able to leverage aspects of liminal space, even when we don't know we're in a period of transition. But what if we could ensure the effectiveness of liminal periods? What if we could not only establish best practices for leveraging liminality to accelerate our growth but also *create* those liminal moments for ourselves?

The ability to craft and manage liminality strategically presents us with unbridled potential. By deftly navigating both the liminal space imposed upon us and the moments we curate, we can accelerate in the direction of our best selves—virtually on demand. The benefit of curated liminality is not the elimination of the unknown per se; it is that knowing when it will happen allows us to optimize the disruption ahead.

Most of us wait for an opening in our lives to pause and weigh our thoughts, behaviors, and goals. We hold off until it's absolutely necessary—often until life decides for us—but what if it were the opposite?

What if you carved out the space and time to consider your current course, your desired trajectory, and whether they align? What if you used those insights to make decisions about where to go next?

---

25   Bruce Feiler, *Life Is in the Transitions: Mastering Change at any Age* (New York: Penguin Press, 2020).

Several years ago, we began carving out think weeks once a quarter to do just that—to get out of our home, our office, our day-to-day hustle and think about where our business had been, where we wanted it to go, and how we'd take it there.

Once, we were sitting in the Cleveland airport waiting for a flight to Iceland, where we'd do our think week. The stranger next to us asked about our travel plans, and we explained the purpose of our trip. "Wow, I wish I could do that," he replied. Since he was on his way to spend a week in the same destination we were headed to, we guessed that he could.

A few months later, we spoke with a pair of business partners who expressed the same sentiment. They said they'd love to do something similar, but they could never get away from the office for that period of time—and certainly not together. But we would argue that they—and the vast majority of us—have it upside down. It's not about looking for elusive opportunities to get away from the work; it's about finding a way to do some of the deepest and most important work of all.

You don't have to go to Iceland to do it, though it certainly helps. It's a place so different from what many of us are familiar with—almost like the moon. The landscape just doesn't sync with back home, and as a result, it opens the window to considering and reconsidering almost everything we know. However, any situation that takes you out of your comfort zone and into unfamiliar circumstances can support that work.

Authors Chip Conley and Ingo Rauth have studied the experiences of those in the middle of their lives, particularly when it comes to lifelong learning, which many are told will help them compete professionally in aggressive work environments. They found that "long life learning" programs, those designed with a focus on "developing a sense of purpose and well-being by understanding the positive aspects of aging congruent with established adult development theories to create more resilience through midlife transitions," are particularly effective in helping midlifers navigate their experiences.[26] If they could understand what they were experiencing at that point in their lives and see its value, they could use it to their advantage.

They write, "American philosopher John Dewey suggested, 'We do not learn *by* experience, we learn *from* experience as we reflect on it and reconstruct it.' But this takes a learning environment in which midlifers 'can leap into the unknown, and a safety net that can catch them if they fall.'"[27] Of course, that logic isn't limited to midlifers. It extends to people of all ages who are looking to master new skills and thrive in unfamiliar environments. All of us can benefit from making the time to not only explore the unknown but also consider what we have learned there.

An Out-of-the-Box Approach to Leadership Development

In early 2020, Amy had the opportunity to enter curated liminality and reconsider her leadership style, leaving her desk behind for a day spent with an equine leadership organization. There, she watched the lead horse corral a team of horses not from the front, but from behind. It was a servant-leadership approach, providing support and energy from the back of the group to make forward progress.

Later, she was tasked with putting what she'd learned to work by leading a horse through an obstacle course. As they began moving through the course, the horse picked up speed. It started to trot, then

---

26   Chip Conley and Ingo Rauth, "The Emergence of Long Life Learning," ResearchGate, September 21, 2020, DOI: 10.13140/RG.2.2.19860.12162.

27   Conley and Rauth, "The Emergence of Long Life Learning."

canter. She had been taught how to stop a horse, but not how to slow one down, and in the moment, the lack of information clouded her consciousness. She began to step in front of the horse as it lumbered forward, attempting to slow it down. Seeing a dangerous situation in the making, the instructor intervened, bringing the horse to a halt with a single command.

"Did you really think that would work?" he asked, looking at her quizzically.

She shook her head. And in that moment, reflecting on how her attempt to lead the horse had gone awry, she thought of her team. She realized how often she got in front of them, attempting to course correct, but preventing them from tapping into their full potential in the process. Right then, she recognized the full power of servant leadership, of providing support from behind.

That experience served as a paradigm shift for her. Amy took that lesson home, back to the familiar surroundings of her work life. She shared the story with her team, and then she began to take it to heart, giving people on her team opportunities they wouldn't have had before—tasks she would have simply taken on herself. She began incorporating more coaching and mentoring into her approach, to truly lead from behind.

From there, she mapped the lesson onto other domains of her existence—parenting, partnership, and more. That—the rapid acquisition of new concepts, a greater understanding of their role in work and life, and insight into how to implement and sustain those lessons—is the power of curated liminality.

A Chance to Tone the Learning Muscle

There are many benefits of curated liminality, particularly for those in leadership roles who are charged with knowing every day. When your job is making the right decisions—what product to launch, the right time frame in which to restructure, how to respond to a big client or a frustrated employee, and more—it can feel difficult, if not impossible, to be in learning mode at work. We are expected to have an answer or to find one immediately if we don't. The curated liminal experience can liberate that learning mindset, which can be a refreshing, healthy, and productive opportunity.

Learning to be a good follower is often a path to understanding how to be a great leader.

These experiences also provide the chance to experience a new role in the leadership-followership continuum. In the remote wilderness of Patagonia, for example, Leadership Venture participants must depend on the experienced guides to keep them safe as they trek across glaciers and through ever-changing weather. For the first time in a long time, they may be in a position where they don't know what they are doing and must rely on someone else to safely reach their goals. That shift can be tremendously productive, as learning to be a good follower is often a path to understanding how to be a great leader.

In addition, when we curate liminal moments for ourselves and incorporate their lessons into our lives—when we develop our emotional, social, and contextual awareness—we are more prepared to leverage the liminal spaces that will inevitably be imposed on us personally and professionally. We are better able to absorb, integrate, and sustain the learning from liminal experiences on the road ahead.

The Four Phases of Curated Liminality

To optimize and absorb the numerous benefits of curated liminality, we have divided it into four phases, the majority of which overlap with liminality at large. The four phases of curated liminality are preparation, catalyst, integration, and sustainability. In the chapters to come, we will take a deep dive into each phase, its respective opportunities, and its potential impact on work and life. But first, we'll run through their progression.

PREPARATION

An intentional period of preparation is the differentiator between curated liminality and the imposed periods of liminality we find ourselves in. Because curated liminality is intentional—you are choosing to enter into liminal space rather than being thrust into it—you have the advantage of being able to prepare. As such, curated experiences allow us to gear up for the challenge ahead and harvest its insights in the best manner possible.

Consider the preparation phase a boot camp, not only for curated liminality but also for life. When you develop this muscle, you ensure you are prepared to respond, rather than react, in any number of circumstances. This phase is fed by emotional and social intelligence, both of which can be honed with a number of tools and exercises that we'll share.

CATALYST

The disruption to routine that is the hallmark of liminal space occurs during the catalyst phase. It opens up your worldview, allowing you to see or experience something differently both during and in the wake of change. The catalyst creates a greater capability for absorption than you had previously. It allows you to shift perspective and reconsider things that you may have seen in a particular light since the beginning of your business, your career, or even your life.

Author and management consultant Margaret Wheatley writes about creating "islands of sanity" for leaders. Catalytic experiences can create that island of sanity. They help us reacquaint ourselves with who we are and who we may want to be as individuals, teams, or entire organizations. They can liberate us from black-and-white thinking, enabling recognition that, in a society that preaches polarity—conservative versus liberal, haves versus have-nots, and more—we can identify and align ourselves with options and solutions that exist on a gradient rather than at extremes.

But the catalyst doesn't have to be a tough hike up a steep hill or an interaction with a two-thousand-pound animal. Those are ways to do it, but they're not the only ones. And often, even if a physical challenge or environmental shift does play a part in creating disruption—it's just one component in a catalytic experience. Upon return from our Leadership Ventures, participants realize that they have had a more emotionally taxing experience than a physically taxing one. And often, they realize they had done far more to prepare physically than they did to prepare emotionally.

With that in mind, much of the philosophy behind curated liminality is built on the value of the cohort. We often call back to an Irish proverb: "Two shorten the road." When we're in a particular situation together, what seems impossible becomes less so. Being able to purposefully enter into liminality with others is another benefit.

INTEGRATION

The first two stages—preparation and catalyst—would be nothing without the next two: integration and sustainability. The value of curated liminality—and liminality at large—also rests on our ability to incorporate what we've learned into our lives and maintain the transformation spurred by those lessons.

The integration stage is about carrying forward what you've learned and remaining open to additional insights that may arise after the fact. After all, it is often days, weeks, or even months after a catalytic experience that something clicks.

Many times, the layers of insight and the capacity for knowing that are built within the catalytic phase are not revealed all at once. Both awe and humility grow over time. You may drink in the magnificence of particular moments of looking at the sky from the depths of the Grand Canyon or the mountains of Patagonia, but it may take years to realize how that moment has changed the way you think and operate in so many different aspects of your life.

You also have the ability to spark that awareness by considering the impact of the catalyst and by asking yourself what you plan to start or stop doing, as well as what you are going to continue to do. Here, we want to make it clear that we are not advocating change for change's sake. If your only takeaway from a catalytic experience is a greater sense of clarity and resolve that you are on the right path, then you've had a tremendous win. Validation is just as important as a deliberate and meaningful change of course.

The integration phase is about considering how the disruption you've experienced might impact other people and elements of your life. That's why a big part of our Leadership Ventures is devoted to re-entry and to recognizing the implications of a changed person going back into an unchanged environment, with individuals who haven't been through the same experience participants have just had. It takes thought and effort to determine how to create synchronicity with people who haven't just had a catalytic experience—and it's also quite important. We often frame this thoughtful reconsideration of the different aspects of our lives as *re-contracting*, and it extends to our beliefs, our behaviors, and our interactions with the other people who play key roles in our worlds.

We also consider integration an alternative to the frequently hyped, but often elusive, concept of balance. Balance implies that you have to give up some of one thing to get more of another, but we find that's not always the case. Many times, different aspects of our existence—whether personal, professional, or both—benefit from being integrated rather than balanced. Integration also provides the opportunity to develop a plan to address any hurdles or obstacles that may arise—including the people or systems that can provide support—and how to mindfully ask for help when it's needed, something the search for balance tends to leave out.

Thus, having a community with which to experience curated liminality is also immensely valuable when it comes to integrating and sustaining lessons learned. It allows for another layer of processing.

There's another significant point to make here as well: You can always determine whether this is actually the right time to integrate. Once you discover something about yourself or your process during or after the catalyst, you can't un-know it, but knowing doesn't mean that knowledge must be integrated right away.

There is value in mindfully choosing whether to integrate or not, depending on your current circumstances. It may be better to sit with your new awareness before incorporating it. And that is a tremendous advantage of curated liminality: the participant always has editorial control. Many times, participants find that less is more—that choosing just a few keystone takeaways is more valuable than attempting to overhaul every aspect of their organization or life.

SUSTAINABILITY

Sustainability, the final phase of liminality, is about living what you've learned every day, keeping it alive and at the forefront of your mind. When what you've learned is sustained, your thoughts, belief system, and behaviors are all in alignment, generating immense power.

emotion ➡ behavior ➡ outcomes

We often talk about the achievement equation, in which emotion drives behavior, which then drives outcomes. Staying rooted in the emotional connection to your why—which becomes evident over the course of the three prior phases—helps maintain these behaviors for the long haul.

The Four Phases in Action

As we explore each phase of curated liminality in more detail, we'd like to tell you a true story. It's about a company's senior executives and their decision to harness the power of curated liminality to recognize the potential of some of their most promising leaders and accelerate their growth. But while the leadership team may have thought they were just launching a powerful new professional development initiative, the participants—and the CEO himself—ended up coming to some surprising conclusions about themselves in the process, conclusions from which we can all learn.

CHAPTER 7

preparation.

This particular story of curated liminality begins not in an exotic or remote location, but in Detroit, Michigan, where Horizon Global, a worldwide manufacturing company serving the automotive aftermarket, is based.

Mark Zeffiro had just been named its president and CEO and was tasked with bringing Horizon Global public as it was spun off from TriMas Corporation, where he had been executive vice president and CFO. Rick had been Mark's coach at TriMas amid a larger leadership and strategic development initiative, and when Mark became CEO of Horizon, telos was brought in to work with him and his leadership team.

One day, Rick got a call from Jason Desentz, Horizon Global's vice president of human resources. Mark was looking for a new way to engage employees around the globe and help them take the next step in their careers. The company had a CEO Award, which they used to recognize high-potential employees, but it just didn't pack the punch—or produce the kind of results—they wanted. Horizon was looking for a way to not only identify and recognize future senior leaders at the company but also provide them with a catalytic experience that would accelerate their trajectory. Jason asked if Rick had any ideas about what that experience could be. Indeed, he did.

Horizon and telos partnered to design and develop a custom Leadership Venture that would bring together a small group of employees from around the world to simultaneously acknowledge their potential and encourage their transformation. They would do it on the Boulder Mail Trail, the stark, awe-inspiring location we described in the previous chapter.

But before embarking on the venture, they would stop in another Southwestern state, Nevada. They would first head to the Specialty Equipment Market Association (SEMA) tradeshow in Las Vegas, which brings together companies and individuals that make, buy, and sell vehicle specialty parts and accessories of all kinds. For these future leaders, the trip would culminate with Horizon's board meeting, which was also set to be held in Las Vegas. Fresh off the trail, the CEO Award recipients would have the opportunity to share their experiences with the board.

Rick would facilitate the trip with Rich McClellan, a director at telos. Jason would join, too, giving him the opportunity to see the venture's impact on the Horizon employees up close—and reflect on his own leadership approach.

One of the guiding philosophies I have is to listen, learn, and then lead. I take time to listen to what I've heard, learn about the particular situation at hand—investigating and doing my due diligence—and finally offer up a form of leadership.

Now, that doesn't mean I just say, "Here's what we're going to do." More often than not, it means introducing questions I'm curious about to let others find their way. This was an opportunity for some of our most promising employees to do that.

We had originally gotten the telos team involved to work with our senior executives, and through that process, I learned about their Leadership Ventures. We already had the CEO Award in existence, but the process didn't quite have teeth to it. Twenty people used to get it, rather than a select few, and it took the form of a plaque and a thank-you, rather than a significant development opportunity. We wanted a process that would be more meaningful and help those with the highest potential step up.

Working with the telos team, we decided to limit the number of recipients to make it more of a development process for a select few into whom we'd invest thought, time, effort, and money.

To maintain its prestige, I didn't want more than five awardees. But rather than pick a specific number, I decided to set up criteria for the process based on our perfor-mance-management system and select those who seemed to be the right fit. After a lot of thought and conversation, we landed on our inaugural group: three employees—all engineers—from offices around the world.

While they were excited, they were also nervous. Hell, I was nervous too. And while we saw them as future leaders of the company, they didn't necessarily see themselves that way, so we asked them to really reflect on that before-hand: What if you had these roles? What do you think the expectations of those roles are? It was one way we had them prepare for the venture itself and for the positions they might take on one day.

We also asked them to prepare for what would definitely be a physical challenge. Leadership Ventures emphasize the mind and body connection, so the body must be ready too.

Before the trip, we knew where we were going. We reviewed a PowerPoint with details about the experience. We completed our physical training. But none of us could have told you what would happen next. It's not unlike the feeling of having kids—you just don't know what to expect.

We flew into Flagstaff, Arizona, and then took a bus to a small town with Mormon roots. People in the manufactur-ing industry like to have a beer at the start of a business trip, and this was no different; it was the first thing we wanted to do when we arrived at our destination. But this town was dry. Already, we found ourselves a bit out of our comfort zone.

From there, we would all break down the barriers to our vulnerability—something these engineers hadn't had much experience with. On the trail, the preparation and reflection they had done up front would come into play.

Honestly, the process ended up being life changing for me too. I'm always on the go, always thinking about my own evolution. Many inflection points in my life have brought me to this point, but the venture allowed me to take a step back, self-reflect on where I am, where I've been, and—most important—how to slow down.

It's become an additional lens through which I look at my life. I try to take everything in and slow my thoughts before I react. Sometimes it works, sometimes it doesn't. But it allows me to reflect on what someone said before proceeding. I had my personal philosophy of leadership—listening, learning, and then leading—before the venture, but the experience reinforced my belief in it.

On the trail, we did something we weren't supposed to do. We took some little stones and built our own set of cairns—the rock stacks on the side of the trail that let you know you're still on the right path—and agreed that we'd each put them on our desks at work. When things got tough, we'd look over at the cairns, reflect on everything we learned during that experience, and draw from it to address the concern in front of us. Those little rocks sit on my desk to this day.

As Jason and his team learned, there's value not only in liminal experiences themselves but also in preparing for them. Think for a minute about those events in your life over which you had no control that helped shape you into who you are today. A layoff that arrived out of nowhere and eventually led you to your true professional passion. A painful breakup that taught you something about your intrinsic value. A shift in organizational leadership that enabled you to take on more responsibility and reach new heights.

Now, consider what the outcome might have been if you had the opportunity to prepare for those moments. Chances are you would have been better able to understand them, put them into context, and ultimately use them to an even greater advantage. In those cases where it seems as if the outcome would have been the same, preparation provides the opportunity to accelerate the speed at which that insight or knowledge can be integrated and sustained. Perhaps a lesson that took years to learn could have been identified and incorporated in just a handful of months.

Preparation helps us reach new heights, better and faster. It is about dialing up our readiness to absorb and benefit from a liminal experience. That level of readiness is an individual measure—we all enter liminality at different points on the readiness continuum—but there is always an opportunity to improve upon our current station.

There are four elements that contribute to effective preparedness: identifying what's enduring, setting an intention, cultivating awareness, and building community.

Identify What's Enduring

The first step in preparation is to identify what is enduring for ourselves. Why? By and large, we're unwilling to change unless we know what won't. Thus, cataloguing the elements of our lives that are enduring—our values, priorities, strengths, weaknesses, and more—serves to build a solid, unchanging foundation from which to make decisions and move forward when everything else seems to be in flux. For example, though the J.M. Smucker Company has undergone significant change in recent years, their core values—many of which were derived from Jerome Smucker's leadership more than a century ago—remain the same and continue to guide their decisions.

Set an Intention

Part of being as ready as possible to absorb a liminal experience is to set an intention for the time you'll spend in liminal space. Prior to embarking on Leadership Ventures, we ask participants to set one or more intentions. We ask them what they hope the destination to which they're headed will teach them. We encourage them to consider the issues on which they hope to gain insight and to pose the questions they want to address. Setting those intentions serves to ready them to take in insights and information during the catalyst.

When you set an intention, you take ownership over your experience. You commit to seeking answers for yourself, rather than waiting for a lightning bolt of knowing to strike. And that's vital, as more often than not seeking and finding take a little bit of framing.

What will the Colorado River or the Mountains of Patagonia or the Canyons of Utah teach you about life's biggest questions? Nothing and everything, all at the same time. The landscape in and of itself teaches you nothing about leadership or operations or relationships, but when you are equipped with a sense of ownership—developed through intention—the environment becomes an invaluable resource for some of those answers.

By the same token, it's crucial to remain aware that what you uncover may be far different from what you had imagined. Often, we see those who have engaged in curated liminality end up with an entirely different takeaway than the one they had set out to find and bring home. Interestingly, though, it's the act of setting those intentions that helps them arrive in a place they may not have ever thought they'd end up. Along with ownership, intention cultivates openness.

In our office, we have a quote from mountaineer and adventurer Rick Ridgeway hanging on our wall. It reads, "The best journeys are the ones that answer questions that at the outset you never even thought to ask." When it comes to curated liminality, that couldn't be truer. Preparation provides the opportunity to understand and embrace that truth. But it's not always easy.

Cultivate Awareness

Before a Leadership Venture begins, participants tend to reach out with requests for more information. They want detailed descriptions of what the terrain is going to be like. They want to know exactly what the temperature is going to be during their trip. Frequently, there's an intensity to their emails and calls; they ask as if we're keeping something from them.

And while they may believe they want and need those answers so they can get the right type of hiking boots or purchase the perfect set of performance clothing, what they really want is to reinforce their perceived sense of control. That's where the intensity comes from. They're asking, "On what day, during which exercise, is the lightning going to strike me?"

We always tell Leadership Venture participants that we are not withholding any information. It's not our goal to restrict visibility. We let them know that there will never be a point in the process where something will jump out from behind them as a form of intervention. But just as they can't know whether their intentions will come to fruition, we cannot in any way provide clarity as to exactly what's going to happen out there—we can't delineate the challenges and epiphanies that will come up moment to moment.

When we explain that, a rich dialogue often arises. We encourage them to examine the intensity with which they request that visibility. What they often realize is that it is a proxy for what's happening at work and at home.

Cultivating that kind of self-awareness is a skill, one that is particularly important, as self-awareness forms the foundation of all meaningful growth. An individual's understanding of their unique strengths emanates from self-awareness as well. To further build skills when it comes to awareness, we provide journaling and mindfulness exercises like the ones you'll find in the appendix. With open-ended exercises like these, Leadership Venture participants begin to understand that in many ways, they are entering into an experience of their own making.

Self-awareness forms the foundation of all meaningful growth.

A MULTIMODAL APPROACH

Our Leadership Ventures—and curated liminality at large—is not about uncovering a series of foolproof steps to great leadership or self-actualization; it's about finding one's own voice and path. On our ventures, we often go off trail. We take the lesser-traveled passageways. Uncovering the right route for you as an individual requires the same type of strategy.

As such, we take a multimodal approach to all our development experiences, employing a wide variety of exercises and activities in each program to help people uncover information and knowledge from within and use it to drive their personal progress. We acknowledge that not everything works for everyone and that it takes a unique cocktail of activities designed to appeal to different learning styles—visual, logical, verbal, aural, and physical—to foster individual self-discovery.

The diversity of programming also encourages participants to use both sides of their brain, leading to richer, deeper understanding. Including these multimodal exercises and activities as part of preparation, before the catalyst takes place, serves as a kind of psychological cross-training that enables them to fully experience and optimize what comes up during the catalyst.

This is especially valuable for leaders who are used to operating from their own set of go-to strategies. Expanding the playbook on the trail or in a coaching session leads to difference-making moves in the office and throughout their lives.

Build Community

To set intentions and cultivate awareness, participants self-select areas of improvement and take full ownership over their past, present, and future success. Ultimately, this methodology lays the foundation for driving meaningful and sustainable improvements in business and in life. But that doesn't mean it can be accomplished alone. Transformation is self-selected, yes. You—and only you—must come to the conclusion that you want or need to change something about your existence. But it is also codirected; it takes reflection with another person or group of people—a tribe, as discussed in chapter 4—to determine what the next right step is.

THE VALUE OF VULNERABILITY-BASED TRUST

In chapter 4, we discussed Patrick Lencioni's concept of vulnerability-based trust: being comfortable enough to quickly acknowledge, without provocation, one's mistakes, weaknesses, failures, and needs

Vulnerability-based trust is the foundation of all successful relationships, but many times, it's a new concept for people.

for help, as well as the strengths of others—even when those strengths exceed your own. Vulnerability-based trust is the foundation of all successful relationships, but many times, it's a new concept for people. They have had plenty of experience with predictive trust—trusting those in their lives simply because they know them well enough to anticipate how they will behave or react—but they haven't learned how to trust openly and vulnerably, without anticipating what others might say or do.

Vulnerability-based trust is an expectation of Leadership Ventures participants. Often, teaching it is as simple as inviting them to be vulnerable for the first time. But in order for the lessons they learn to stick, they must build vulnerability-based trust into their existing relationships at work and at home.

Before a Leadership Venture, we recommend exercises for participants to build vulnerability-based trust with their coach and other key people in their lives, so that if and when they need help, they are able to reach out. One of those exercises involves asking the most important people in their lives to write them a letter prior to their departure. They won't open it until day three of the venture, when they are well into the catalyst, but the request itself has preparatory value. They are engaging those who matter most—their community—as a mechanism of support as they ready themselves to participate in what is inevitably going to be a challenge.

APPLYING A SYSTEMS-BASED APPROACH FOR GREATER IMPACT

The act of building community is representative of our systems-based approach. Systems thinking refers to the perspective that there are multiple relationships at play in any particular situation—including connections between individuals or outcomes that may seem entirely unrelated at first.[28] To further clarify, Peter Senge, a senior lecturer at MIT and founding chair of the Society for Organizational Learning, breaks down systems and their impact by explaining that families are a kind of system, one that each of us operates within. Importantly, even a system as simple as a family has complexities that create undesirable outcomes.[29]

With that in mind, we begin every engagement by taking into account how individual components of the organization (leader, team, etc.) relate to each other, as well as the ways in which these individual components work over time and within the context of the organization. Taking this tack expands the range of choices available in solving a problem by broadening our thinking and helping us articulate problems in new and different ways. The same goes for engaging a community—we prepare not just the individual for a liminal experi-

---

28 "Peter Senge: Learning Organizations and Systems Thinking:" study.com, https://study.com/academy/lesson/peter-senge-learning-organizations-systems-thinking.html#:~:text=According%20to%20Senge%2C%20learning%20organizations,integrates%20with%20all%20the%20others

29 "Peter Senge Introduction to Systems Thinking," YouTube video, 2:20, posted by Kris Wile, August 5, 2014, https://www.youtube.com/watch?v=eXdzKBWDraM

ence but also the ecosystem around them, so that when they return, they have a network of people who can work with them to confidently navigate the road ahead, no matter what comes up.

TRUE COLLABORATION STEMS FROM SUPPORT AND CHALLENGE

The effort to build community up front also reflects our core belief that true collaboration stems from both support and challenge. The first step toward true collaboration is seeing individuals, teams, departments, and other functional areas as an interconnected ecosystem requiring collaborative approaches to mobilize staff, partners, and customers around a common purpose. Collaboration demands working together to achieve a common goal by participating in conversations, meetings, and interactions both passively (i.e., only listening and learning) and actively (i.e., contributing to the group). Further, true collaboration means challenging the status quo and, when necessary, engaging in healthy conflict with respect and transparency.

When it comes to effectively navigating challenge, we can look to coauthors of *The Leadership Challenge* by James Kouzes and Barry Posner for insight. They interviewed thousands of people across genders, cultures, ages, and numerous other traits on their peak leadership experiences. They found that there were five common behavior patterns among all of these leadership success stories. Kouzes and Posner described these core practices as Modeling the Way, Inspiring a Shared Vision, Challenging the Process, Enabling Others to Act, and Encouraging the Heart. In Challenging the Process, "leaders search for opportunities to change the status quo. They look for innovative ways to improve the organization. In doing so, they experiment and take risks."[30]

In addition, to counter the potential to become overwhelmed, and to be somewhat paralyzed as a result, leaders must foster and recognize small wins by setting interim goals on the way toward achieving larger objectives, limit action-preventing bureaucracy, and accept mistakes and failures as learning opportunities.[31] Establishing these guidelines at the outset of a Leadership Venture allows individuals to engage in true collaboration and better manage challenges upon their return, bolstered by everything they have learned during the catalyst.

So, how do you know when your preparation is complete—when you're truly ready to move on to the catalyst? It all comes down to intention. Considering what you hope to learn from your surroundings, cultivating awareness, and building a community to provide support in liminal space and beyond are deliberate efforts that allow you to take advantage of the full value of the catalyst.

Curated Liminality on and off the Trail

Before we move on, we want to remind you that curated liminality and its four stages have applications to numerous experiences, not just those facilitated by visiting a far-flung locale. As we mentioned, while Leadership Ventures remain our most immersive expression of curated liminality, we incorporate the philosophies of curated liminality into every engagement we have, including individual and team-based coaching.

---

30   "This Is What It Means to Lead," leadershipchallenge.com, https://www.leadership-challenge.com/research/five-practices.aspx

31   "This Is What It Means to Lead."

By definition, coaching takes place in liminal space, as it falls outside the hierarchy of the organization. To further drive that discontinuity, most coaching sessions happen outside participants' offices, whether in a park or coffee shop, or at an art museum, yoga studio, or cooking class—we'll do almost anything to get people out of the norm and out of their heads.

During one exercise, a team was tasked with finding pieces of art in their local museum that represented different values embodied by the organization. In another, hospital employees toured their own facilities with the goal of taking photographs (HIPAA compliant, of course) that embodied the organization's purpose. For both groups, flipping the script on their typical coaching and leadership training experiences was immensely powerful.

We also engage a coachee's community, interviewing six to eight of the individuals who work with them, and ask them to determine how the lessons the coachee learns could potentially have an impact on the team they are on, the team they lead, their organization as a whole—even their family. It's another example of our systems-based approach in action.

And to operationalize the collaboration piece in a coaching environment, we invite the coachee to engage in an advocate meeting, bringing along someone they view as a trusted and enduring advocate for them, personally and professionally. The coach brings their own advocate as well, establishing a four-way dialogue about what it means to truly advocate for each other. It's a rich part of the process that further bolsters trust, systems, and multimodal learning.

With that in mind, as we continue to unpack the Horizon team's experience, know that you can engage in and reap the many benefits of curated liminality in a variety of environments and circumstances simply by choosing to deviate from the status quo. You don't have to wait for a seemingly transformative moment, either. In fact, you can start to spur transformation on your own, right now. We've included exercises in the appendix to help you do just that. Completing them as they appear will prime you to best absorb the next set of insights.

APPENDIX EXERCISES FOR THE PREPARATION PHASE

- Balance Wheel
- My Gift
- My Values

CHAPTER 8

catalyst.

You know by now that the concept of liminal space is predicated on the power of the in between: periods that allow—or even require—us to consider everything we thought we knew about ourselves, our businesses, and even life itself. Liminal space is marked by a catalyst: a disruption in our daily lives or way of being that thrusts us into the unknown. What might those catalysts look like, particularly when you are crafting them on your own?

For example, those who choose to participate in any of our Leadership Ventures are creating a catalytic experience for themselves, one with the potential to launch them into a period of liminality that stretches long beyond their time with us. And they do it by willingly engaging in a disruptive experience they wouldn't otherwise have. For example, more than 5 million people visit the Grand Canyon each year. Fewer than 2 percent of them ever take a step below the rim. Fewer than 1 percent ever

> **Liminal space is marked by a catalyst: a disruption in our daily lives or way of being that thrusts us into the unknown.**

spend the night there. And even fewer actually dip their toe in the Colorado River at its base. Participants on our Grand Canyon Leadership Venture engage in all those experiences and more—the kind that go beyond a family vacation or an office-wide retreat—to trigger transformation. This is a true 1 percent experience for those who are, or aspire to be, a top 1 percent performer in their given domain.

The benefit of curating liminality yourself is that there is no uncertainty surrounding the existence or time frame of the catalyst. You orchestrate your own immersion into the unknown. As a result, the catalyst has the potential to be more efficient and impactful when you choose it for yourself than if you were to find yourself navigating an unexpected catalytic experience.

Rich McClellan has led numerous groups into liminal space over the course of his life and career—including the Boulder Mail Trail venture the Horizon team took. Here, he shares his perspective on the power of catalytic experiences in initiating liminality—and the challenges that present when we find ourselves back in familiar territory.

I remember the first conversations Rick, Amy, and I had about the notion of liminality and helping people access it through Leadership Ventures. The concept resonated with me immediately. Throughout my life, I'd had experiences with a liminal quality to them.

I was a Boy Scout as a kid. Each year, my troop set out on high adventure trips. One summer, we rode our bicycles from Cleveland, Ohio, to upstate New York. Another summer, we built our own kayaks, taking them down the Allegheny River for a couple of weeks. As I got older, I continued to seek out experiences like these.

In college, I took a class—cross-listed between the English and sports and recreation departments—called "Wilderness Writing." Every weekend, we'd take a trip. We went snowshoeing and built igloos, hiked through Zion's Narrows in southern Utah—things like that. While we were on those trips, we'd write. They served as periods of reflection and introspection.

As an adult, I led Mormon youth groups, reenacting our pioneer heritage of crossing the plains. With fifteen teenagers, I would spend a week pulling a handcart loaded with our belongings for twenty miles or so—just as our ancestors did. One time, we traveled along the Cuyahoga Scenic Railroad. Another, we forded a river with water raging up to our chests. On that trip, we actually ended up getting evacuated at three in the morning, during a torrential downpour.

Even then, I noted the difference between the two experiences. The one in which we traveled on the railroad bed had nowhere near the level of impact on me as the one in which I forged the river and encountered all those physical challenges. Afterward, I realized that as Americans we live in a luxurious society. Most of us are cushioned from so many real challenges. I've read diaries from ancestors who lived 150 or 200 years ago and wrote passages like, "We went down to Annie's wedding, and Bob fell off his horse and died." Today, you don't run nearly as high a risk of dying at a wedding—that's certainly a plus. But with such a comfortable existence, there are also elements of risk and challenge that many of us are missing out on.

Our lives have become quite soft. We're not used to having the kinds of experiences that force us to confront some very real challenges and face risk head on. But that's what Leadership Ventures do. And having been lucky enough to have experiences like that throughout my life, it didn't take much explaining on Rick and Amy's part for me to grasp their power.

There are several core principles that make these experiences so impactful. One is creating a certain distance from our normal lives, physically, mentally, emotionally, or otherwise. Just as the prophets would climb a mountain to see God, we have to get away from normal life in order to have a deep, personal, spiritual experience. Another is rigor. The experience doesn't have to break you, but you must be challenged in multiple ways.

For many people, the lip of the Grand Canyon serves as the catalyst for their liminal experience, not because of the physical challenge that lies ahead, but because of the heights. You can see them go into emotional lockdown, their bodies freezing as they look out over the rocky ledges.

I'm actually terrified of heights. The first time I hiked the Grand Canyon, I knew that would be my issue. It's something that still bothers me today—I have to go to my happy place to process it. But having to face up to some of the fears and apparent physical limitations we have is what makes a curated liminal experience possible. We are putting the ingredients together to create liminality.

Another key aspect is the emotional and digital separation. Six, seven, or eight days without a phone or email really makes a difference. We find that on Leadership Ventures, it takes about three or four days before people truly become present.

The awe-inspiring scenery adds to the experience as well, helping to drive home a particularly powerful paradox— one highlighted in the book *The Man Who Walked Through Time*, by Colin Fletcher. It is recommended reading for all our Grand Canyon trekkers. In it, Fletcher discusses the paradox between feeling as if you have infinite potential and simultaneously that you are absolutely nothing. The Grand Canyon is a great place to remember that. You're so far removed from anything human. You're looking at this overwhelmingly beautiful landscape, and as you get down to the bottom, you find yourself standing in a one-and-a-half-billion-year-old range of rock.

Right then, you think, "Wow, I'm just here for a split second. That's all I've got compared to these rocks." And at the same time, there's the sense that this is also your life. That you can do what you want with it. You can liberate yourself. There is greatness within you, and you can achieve eternal things. That's humbling to realize.

A good coach will tell you that sometimes you can see in someone's eyes when something has clicked. Maybe they forgave themselves for something they've never been able to forgive themselves for before, let go of something that was holding them back, or committed to do something different in the future. As a coach, I get to see those moments happen live. On a Leadership Venture, I get to see them emerging all day, every day.

On this particular trip with Horizon's team members, I saw numerous catalytic moments unfold. On the Boulder Mail Trail, there are endless rolling rock hills that seem to blend into one another. If you're not careful, it's easy to lose your bearings—there's nothing out there to give you a sense of where you're heading. Of course, our guides had been through this passage many times before. They knew where we were. But there were a couple of times when they had to turn around and backtrack because they had lost the cairns—those stacks of rocks that let you know you're still on the trail. The participants began realizing how the guides were staying on track, that the cairns made life easy, pointing them in the right direction.

That became a great metaphor for one member of the group. He realized that, on the trail and in life, he just needed to figure out what his next cairn would be, where it was, what it was pointing toward, and how he'd get from here to there. As long as he could do that—as long as he could say, "Okay, where's my next cairn?"—he was going to be okay.

At that time, he was facing a lot of uncertainty at work. The company had just promoted him, but at the same time they were conducting mass layoffs, and now he was responsible for shutting down factories and firing hundreds of people. On the one hand, his responsibilities and pay were going up, and on the other, he was having to downsize and exit people he cared about. That made for a very challenging personal and professional experience. But the concept of the cairns provided some comfort and resolution: as long as he had his cairns—as long as he knew where he was going—he was good.

We also engage participants in another exercise. It's based on a book we have used for many of our ventures called The Power of Full Engagement by Jim Loehr and Tony Schwartz. In it, the authors detail four different dimensions in which we exist: emotional, mental, physical, and spiritual. They state that, by activating the dimensions we tend to overlook, we allow ourselves to rest the others. Further, to strengthen all four dimensions, we must deliberately and regularly engage with them.

To bring that message to life, we have participants rate their level of activation across each of the four dimensions. They rate themselves at the beginning of the week and again at the end. While those dimensions tend to change over the course of the venture, when most people reflect on what their daily work lives look like, they see that the intellectual elements tend to be overemphasized, that physical elements usually get attention too, but that most of us don't do much when it comes to the emotional and to the spiritual.

On the venture, we also highlight the reality that, typically, we only activate one of those dimensions at a time. We may tap into that emotional dimension by spending time with a friend who is suffering or access our spiritual side by going to a place of worship, but most of us don't do these things on a daily basis. Leadership Ventures have the potential to access multiple dimensions simultaneously. It's challenging to experience even two of those dimensions at a time, and that challenge opens up the space for self-realization.

To me, that's the secret sauce: activating multiple dimensions simultaneously so that while people are thinking about what they can do better, they're experiencing—and expressing—deep, personal emotions about themselves and others. They are reaching out with empathy toward one another. And they are also extremely tired, because they have just hiked ten miles with forty-pound packs on their backs. That's a recipe for an impactful catalyst.

There was another particularly powerful moment for many on that trip. As part of the process, we have participants bring a letter from someone at home. There are no rules about the letter other than that. We don't tell them whom it has to be from, other than that it should be someone close to them. The only other instruction we provide is that, in the letter, the writer should tell the recipient what they want them to know while they're on the trail—and that it should be sealed. That sealed letter travels with them in their pack for some time.

Several days into the trip, as evening begins to fall, we find a great lookout spot. There, surrounded by an amazing view—scenery that reminds participants how human they are and how beautiful the world is—we have them open the letters.

In the letters, they receive reassurances from home that they're loved, that they're good people, and that they're doing the right kinds of things. The letters hold the sorts of message many people don't hear often enough. Perhaps we've done all this curating to get them to this exact moment of vulnerability, to give them this lifeline back to the people who love them the most—and to their own potential.

The exercise also helps us turn the corner in a Leadership Venture. With the catalyst working its magic, we begin to talk to them about what we call "re-entry." To explain what it's like to re-enter the world after an experience like this, I'll tell you about a re-entry experience I had as a teenager.

I had gone off to a youth camp and had a really special, spiritual experience while I was away. I learned a lot about myself. I came home on this high. And then I walked into my house.

I came in through the garage into the kitchen. I'm one of six children, five of whom are boys. All hell had broken loose. Two of my brothers had begun a fistfight. My sister was screaming at another brother. My dad was trying to calm everyone down, demanding that they all just shut up and be nice to one another. In that moment, the feeling— the high from my week learning about myself and all the goodness out there in the world—seemed to evaporate.

That's not uncommon as you come down from an experience like the one a Leadership Venture provides, where you have been wired for deep introspection. While you've been away, everyone else has gone on with their normal lives; nothing has really changed for them. Sometimes, they may even resent the fact that you have been gone on some unconscious level. You're overflowing with enthusiasm for what you've just been through, and they may not have the capacity or interest to absorb all that. Thus, re-entry can be painful and disorienting. One Horizon team member said it took his wife four days to ask how the venture had been. In the end, though, he was happy that she did.

While navigating relationships at home during re-entry may be challenging, those made on the trip are never the same. You establish a closeness, a deep understanding and level of respect for those you've traveled with—learning things about them that you probably wouldn't have discovered otherwise. Just as the catalyst launches one into liminal space, it also serves as an ideal place to accelerate the team formation process. Why? It levels the playing field, while creating new relationships and bonds.

One of the best parts about Leadership Ventures is what they do to common societal hierarchies and to our assumptions about ourselves. I always enjoy watching the typical alpha male during an experience like this. They often come in with a set of assumptions about how they're the boss, the strongest, the one whom everyone else respects. Then, a day in when they've twisted an ankle and can't carry their own backpack, there's a totally different dynamic at play. Humility enters the picture. And surprisingly enough, so has love. You see that playing field level before your eyes—or even shift entirely. That's part of the magic of the catalyst too.

What Constitutes a Catalyst?

Our Leadership Ventures employ physical disruptions to help kick off participants' liminal experiences. But we've already explained that while physical challenges—difficult hikes at high elevations, for example—are certainly an effective way to launch one into liminal space, they're not the only way to do it. Catalytic experiences aren't always physically difficult or aspirational, the way one may view a Leadership Venture. Ultimately, they're about breaking a pattern.

THE THREE-DAY EFFECT

Rich talks about the power of physical and emotional separation, an automatic pattern breaker, that occurs on our ventures. We notice that it takes our participants a few days to sink into the present moment. This observation is backed by the "three-day effect," a concept coined by Ken Sanders, a Utah-based rare-book seller and frequent river rafter.

Years ago, he guided river-rafting trips down the Colorado and Green Rivers and found that, after about three days on the water, he saw a shift in those with whom he traveled.[32]

He discussed his findings with David Strayer, a cognitive neuroscientist at the University of Utah. Strayer responded that he had noticed something similar himself on backpacking trips: "Having hiked around the desert for years, I noticed in myself, and from talking to others, that people think differently after being out in the desert. Their thoughts are clearer; they're certainly more relaxed; they report being more creative … If you can disconnect and experience being in the moment for two or three days, it seems to produce a difference in qualitative thinking."

---

32   Florence Williams, "The Nature Fix: The Three-Day Effect," REI Co-op Journal, https://www.rei.com/blog/camp/the-nature-fix-the-three-day-effect.

In 2012, he launched a study to determine what exactly happened to the brain after three days in nature. He and two colleagues, Paul and Ruth Ann Atchley of the University of Kansas, gave twenty-eight individuals a word-test game called the Remote Associates Test (RAT), which measures creative thinking and insight problem solving, both before and after a backpacking trip. They performed 47 percent better after they returned.

What accounted for the improvement? Strayer posited that, while they were away from the everyday demands of their regular existence, the backpackers' frontal cortex—which handles executive function—had the opportunity to take a break for once. With some much-needed rest, other, more creative areas could take over and become sharper.

Later, Frank Ferraro III, a researcher at the University of Nebraska, was able to replicate the results, having given the RAT to college students before and after a six-day canoe trip. He saw a 50 percent improvement in their scores after the trip.

Ken Sanders sums it up nicely: "I think it takes the first two days and nights to wash away whatever veneer of civilization you have brought with you. The new reality begins on that third day."[33]

CREATING A CRISIS

As humans, we are pattern-recognition and mimicking machines. That's one of the reasons change is so hard. We find comfort in the familiar. When we're operating within the status quo, it feels as if there is no reason to accept or incorporate new ideas. But in a cold-bucket-of-water-type environment, *everything* is changing, making it much easier to adopt a new strategy. That's why breaking that pattern is so

---

33 Williams, "The Nature Fix."

effective. Or, as leadership expert and author John Kotter explains in his book, *A Sense of Urgency*, creating a crisis.[34]

Kotter clarifies that a crisis can also serve as a call to arms, allowing for urgent—and focused—action. Such an event can serve not only as a motivator but also as reassurance that one has the capacity to handle the task at hand—and identify opportunities within.[35] There are countless ways to do that.

At telos, we are in the process of developing shorter experiences called Liminal Intensives. Like our Leadership Ventures, they will employ pattern-breaking catalytic

As humans, we are pattern-recognition and mimicking machines. That's one of the reasons change is so hard.

elements—but on a smaller scale. Liminal Intensives may take the form of a single day spent in nature or in silence. They will demonstrate to participants that launching themselves into liminal space doesn't always require complete detachment from the world with which they are familiar.

And a catalyst can have an even smaller footprint than a daylong retreat—something as simple as switching up your morning routine, spending the day on your feet if you typically sit, or working from home or a coffee shop if you usually come into the office can have a significant impact.

To spur transformation within your organization, you may move teams and individuals to new seats in your office—scattering them throughout your building or bringing them together. You may find that relocating to another building when you find yourself running

---

34   John P. Kotter, *A Sense of Urgency*, (Boston: Harvard Business Press, 2008).

35   Kotter, *A Sense of Urgency*

out of space is an effective catalyst, as one of our clients discovered. The options are endless.

We have begun to incorporate study halls into the beginning of our coaching sessions—another strategy with catalytic implications. The idea came from Edward Tufte, an American statistician and professor at Yale, who believes that every meeting should begin with a study hall and a printed document. He holds that doing so allows for better comprehension of the subject at hand and a more effective session overall. We find it also acts as a disruption—ironically in the form of a moment of calm—when coachees can pause, take a full inhale and exhale, get grounded, and use that moment to thoughtfully begin the work ahead.

We can look to the natural world for an abundance of examples of the power of small shifts. A slight change in temperature transforms gas to liquid and liquid to solid: overwhelming physical transformation rendered within a single degree. A slight shift in hormones kicks off the metamorphosis from caterpillar to butterfly. Catalysts represent leverage in action. That's what makes them so powerful. Ask yourself which shifts—which breaks in the pattern—can yield the same transformative shift in you. It may be as simple as using the transitions that occur in natural spaces for your own reflection and learning. For example, you may want to try journaling as the sun rises, using the time between night and day or doing some thinking while standing on the beach at the edge of the tide, where water meets land.

Acknowledging the Importance of Individual Experience

With the diversity of catalytic possibilities in mind, we must also note that an inherent part of identifying an effective catalyst is recognizing the importance of individual experience. We find that, on a Leadership Venture, the catalyst actually begins at different points for different people.

For those who have never been backpacking before, it may begin when they stand in the middle of a camping store for the first time, attempting to select which gear to buy. For people who have never been away from their children for more than a few days, it may start when they first get on the plane, knowing that they won't see their families for a full week. For others, the catalyst starts when they are standing in a hotel conference room shortly after landing in a new place, engaging in community-building exercises among the individuals with whom they'll spend the next week.

The bottom line is what works to catalyze liminal space for one person may not do so for you. For example, one CEO from Phoenix, Arizona, approached us about doing a Leadership Venture in the Grand Canyon. He often hiked the Grand Canyon and the surrounding area, making the landscape as familiar to him as his own backyard. For him, that experience would not have served as a catalyst. The goal in curating liminal space is to find the right accelerating component for *you*.

How do you know if an experience actually has the potential to serve as a catalyst for you?

Ask yourself:

- Does it feel like a stretch?

- Is it disruptive—does it interrupt or break my pattern?

If not, you likely have some more searching to do.

When It Comes to the Catalyst, Proper Context Is Key

It's not just about finding the right catalyst; it's also about putting the experience into its proper context. For example, Rick was chatting with the members of a chapter of Young Presidents Organization, or YPO, a global group of hard-charging entrepreneurs looking for their next challenge. The group was planning to run the Berlin marathon as the latest endurance test in a series of similar events they had participated in. With each sign-up, they hoped to catalyze significant transformation for their members, but they always returned somewhat unfulfilled. Nothing had the game-changing impact they were looking for.

Why? Marathons and other significant physical feats—climbing Everest or Mount Kilimanjaro, for example—come with a certain sex appeal. With the promise of danger and disruption, they seem to have the makings of a catalytic experience. But in truth, the context matters more than the catalyst itself. Without a strategy to process and contextualize the out-of-the-box experiences in which they participated, the YPO members couldn't effectively launch themselves into liminal space.

While they understood the value of creating a crisis, they failed to harness Winston Churchill's advice on the subject, to "Never let a good crisis go to waste." He made the statement as he worked to form the United Nations and as World War II neared its end. It was his ability to not just recognize a catalyst but also *embrace* and *leverage* it that led to the creation of the UN. That leverage requires breaking down and integrating those disruptive experiences; the value depends on what you do with the time and space that comes after, as you'll see in the next chapter.

APPENDIX EXERCISE FOR THE CATALYST PHASE

- Crafting a Personal Vision

CHAPTER 9

integration.

In his extraordinary book *Man's Search for Meaning*, neurologist, psychiatrist, and Holocaust survivor Viktor Frankl wrote, "Between stimulus and response there is a space. In that space is our power to choose our response. In our response lies our growth and our freedom."[36] For us, curated liminality is a macro-level stimulus that liberates the choicefulness, growth, and resulting freedom that Frankl so eloquently invited us to consider decades ago. And as we begin our discussion of the integration phase, which sits between the catalyst (or stimulus) and sustainability—or the ongoing efforts to uphold and embody that which is learned during liminal space—his words feel particularly poignant.

Integration provides an opportunity to fully evaluate what we've learned, understand its potential to elicit productive and powerful change in numerous facets of our worlds, and identify how best to weave those lessons into our lives.

---

36   Viktor E. Frankl, *Man's Search for Meaning: An Introduction to Logotherapy*, (New York: Simon & Schuster, 1984).

On the Boulder Mail Trail, Fred Brickley, one of Horizon's team members, would find himself grappling with his relationship to work, home, and his family and what that meant for his future.

I was pretty surprised when I got the call. In fact, I didn't even answer the phone the first time. My boss actually had to tell me that I had to take the next call that came through. The second time the phone rang, I answered, and Horizon's CEO was on the other line. I was surprised and honored to receive the CEO Award, to know that Horizon saw how much time and effort I was putting into both the growth of the company and my career. But I also didn't know what to expect from the reward itself: a telos Leadership Venture.

It was when I began the preparation exercises that I started to understand not only what this opportunity would be like but also that it would be a true experience of internal growth.

Two years before I learned I had gotten the award, I had moved my family from the west side of the state to the east side for a job at Horizon. They were supportive, seeing it as a great opportunity, and together we embraced the adventure ahead and uprooted our lives to make the move.

The move came with significant change for them too. The environment was totally different, much more populated than the rural setting they were used to. My wife changed jobs when I did, too, since she couldn't commute from across the state. And my kids started over in a new school.

I was very dedicated to the initiative I had been tasked with leading at work, and it was the great results we had achieved that led to the award. But I also knew that, rather than using the Leadership Venture as a professional development exercise, I wanted to use it to determine what was important to me, what was motivating me, what I would consider satisfaction, and how I would justify wins or losses and to make sure that I had the right priorities in mind. Going into it, I didn't focus on my work as much as on building a deep understanding of why I get out of bed every morning.

The catalyst itself was engaging. Every day, we spent time thinking about a particular theme that influenced our thought process—how it affected us, what it meant to us. Even though I was with a group, I had so much time to be in my own head—taking everything in and checking out of reality to focus on my internal processes.

I found the process very empowering. I've always been a high achiever and very competition-driven, but for the first time, rather than focusing on trying to win or succeed, I dug into my why. If I win, am I going to be able to enjoy it? Will I find more than just the feeling of achieving something? Am I going to be happy that I achieved it? Am I happy with my victories and accomplishments and with the way I'm measuring success?

Those factors have shifted for me since the trek. I had always been driven by numbers and results, but now success has a much softer definition. At work, I want to make sure that we're winning and that we feel good about winning, sure. But I'm also concerned that we're accomplishing what we wanted to accomplish, that we didn't budge on any of the things that were most important to us, and that at the end of the day we can feel like we did everything we wanted to do.

In one exercise, we created symbols of something in our lives that we wanted to get rid of. We thought through why we had decided to let go of it and essentially left it on the trail. Everyone has memories, grudges, or habits that they would like to stop dwelling on or get over—and I had the chance to do that.

I also appreciated the opportunity to think about the things in my life that mean something to me, what I wanted to work on, and the ways in which I wanted to grow. For me personally, I wanted to make sure I was re-embracing the balance of work and family life.

Being away from my wife and kids—the people I see every day—who represent why I exist and why I do what I do, also had a significant impact on me. It's different when you're travelling for work and you talk to them at night or get texts here or there. To not communicate at all with anyone who represents your existence feels pretty strange, but also awesome. In the absence of our communication, our connection only grew. I got to focus on how important they were to me. That was one of the big takeaways for me.

Obviously on the venture we did a big thing physically. We had a lot of bonding time with the others and got to understand what each person was going through. I got really close with the other people from Horizon. I built relationships with individuals from across the globe, and we still check in personally and professionally. But more than anything, I thought about the move.

I thought a lot about what it meant for myself and my family to move away from our close relatives. Was it the right thing to do? How was I handling it? What had I become better at for making the decision to do it— for taking a leap of faith and taking responsibility for a brand-new group of individuals in another location?

In those two years at Horizon, I had grown a lot—much more than I had in the many years that preceded it, as I climbed the professional ladder. But I wasn't sure about whether my work-life balance was where I wanted it to be. At the time, my mother was elderly and sick, and I wanted to ensure I was embracing all the moments I could with her, spending quality time and creating rituals and touch points to keep in contact.

I realized that, while I was glad I made the move and did the things I did, it might not be what I wanted to do—or where I wanted to be—long term. I wasn't sure I was prioritizing what was most important.

I thought about whether I was doing something I wanted to make compromises for and continue to change our lives to participate in. Or did I want to continue to leverage my strengths and move on to a position where I'd have the freedom to operate in a way I felt I performed best, while honoring the other priorities in my life?

Since then, I've done a complete one-eighty and moved back to the west side of the state, back to our old residence, back into the same school system my kids had been in. I realized that was most important for my family from a growth standpoint and a security standpoint.

I also changed jobs, finding a position at a company that still fits my style. Today, I'm working with a group of high achievers in an operation that values competition, strategy, research and development, and new technology. I also spend fewer hours working and commuting. I have more time to be plugged into my community and to do more for others—a big aspect of my life that I felt was missing in my previous role due to the time commitment alone. Now, I have more time to spend with and support my loved ones too.

The Leadership Venture truly allowed me to reflect on what I wanted—and what I thought was important. It was probably what ultimately brought me back to my side of the state. The change has been great for me.

In addition to recognizing the pillars of what makes me happy and why—and the importance of not sacrificing those things—I also learned the importance of prioritizing the behaviors and connections that matter most. I continue to think about the value of forming rituals and connectivity. If something is important to you, you have to make it a priority to do something about it on a regular basis.

Today, I take the same approach with the individuals and teams I manage. I make sure I understand what their end goals are and what and where they want to be—and I do my best to help them get there. Do they want to be a technical leader? Do they want to be a people leader? Are they motivated by competition? Are they motivated by success? By encouragement? I consider the factors that make them happy and why they do what they do, and I use that insight to optimize their experience working with me—and for themselves.

Re-Contracting

Before we get into the details of integration, we must talk about a powerful notion that played a significant role in Fred's Leadership Venture experience. It often arises between the catalyst and integration—a bridge of sorts, bringing us from disruptive or pattern-breaking moments into the weeds of grappling with what we've learned and what we want. We call it re-contracting. Re-contracting is a productive framework in which to consider how we want to integrate what we experience and begin to learn during the catalyst into the rest of our lives.

On every Leadership Venture we run, we start a conversation with participants about how they want to re-contract with different aspects of their lives: their financial selves, their professional selves, the person they tend to show up as in their relationships, and more. Here's a simple example: You may have an unwritten contract governing your relationship to food that states that you've earned the right to have dessert after dinner. But if your weight starts to creep up or health issues begin to arise, you may find you need a new contract that better supports your health. Fred spent a lot of time, both on and off the trail, considering his relationships—particularly those with work and with his family—to determine which contracts were working and which weren't.

While catalytic experiences are about experimentation—beginning to understand and play with how we think or act during a new or challenging situation—the pivot to integration happens when we determine the kinds of behaviors or responses we want to maintain in the long run.

It's not uncommon to become stuck in the beauty and bewilderment of the catalyst, unable to determine how to process what we've experienced and what should come next. In most cases, re-contracting is what's missing.

Why do we refer to it as "re-contracting," rather than simply "contracting"? We all have contracts in various areas of our lives. We have relationships with food, money, information, family, colleagues, friends, our jobs, and so much more. Whether or not we are aware of the specific contracts we have created, they exist. Re-contracting provides the chance to make explicit what has already been implicit for most of us or to reevaluate and redraft implicit contracts.

Moreover, re-contracting allows us to consider multiple possibilities to identify the best possible option. You may be moving an inch in one direction, when three inches in the complete opposite direction may actually be more productive or bring you closer to your goals. For example, in 2020, many families found themselves implementing new contracts as they faced an imposed catalyst: the threat of COVID-19. As schools closed and offices went online, some determined that maintaining an academic schedule similar to what their children had at school was the best possible strategy. Other families took some time to reflect, allowing three or five days to experience this shift together as a family *and then* began considering what re-engaging with schoolwork might look like. Taking the time to consider the options, think about which may be the most productive and engaging for them as individuals and as families—in other words, fully leaning into liminal space—gave them the opportunity to unleash its power through re-contracting and to truly thrive in this new normal. Of course, maintaining that original schedule may be the perfect decision for some, but it is fully marinating in the possibilities that provides the best opportunity for transformative change.

Teams and organizations can also engage in the process of re-contracting, reexamining their relationships to strategy, leadership, collaboration, and to each other, in any area that can benefit from additional intention and clarity.

As we continue our exploration of integration, keep in mind that the catalyst is about becoming aware that those contracts already exist—whether you've been aware of them in the past or not. Integration begins when you make decisions about what they'll look like going forward.

Putting Awareness to Work

Integration—a mindful and deliberate step in harvesting the insights that come amid a catalytic experience—is the phase that is most often missed, whether navigating an imposed or curated period of liminality. With that in mind, we'll provide a framework to help you organize, prioritize, and begin to put your awareness to work. There are a few steps necessary to do that.

INTENTIONAL CHANGE THEORY

First, we can turn to Richard Boyatzis, an organizational theorist and Distinguished University Professor of Organizational Behavior, Psychology, and Cognitive Science at Case Western Reserve University. An expert in emotional intelligence, behavioral change, and competence, he developed Intentional Change Theory, which states that there are five simple steps necessary to cultivate real change.[37]

- Discovering your ideal self—the person you wish to be.

- Discovering your real self—the person you are as of this moment.

---

37 "Intentional Change Theory," Weatherhead School of Management, Case Western Reserve University, https://weatherhead.case.edu/core-topics/intentional-change-theory#:~:text=Core%20Topics-,Intentional%20Change%20Theory,Discover%20your%20real%20self

- Creating your learning agenda—the work you must do to embody the traits of your ideal self.

- Experimenting and practicing new habits.

- Getting support.[38]

The steps are relatively straightforward, and as you read on, we invite you to reflect on the ways in which each of these steps comes into play in the integration phase.

MAKING MEANING FROM THE LESSONS AT HAND

At the outset of the integration phase, we make meaning out of what we have just become aware of. We ask ourselves, What did I learn? Is it truly new or different information than what I had been aware of previously? Does it make sense to me? What does it mean? How does it align with who I am and who I want to be? How do I integrate that into my life? With those questions answered, we can begin to sort our insights into meaning-making buckets that can inform our priorities and actions. To do that, we must develop a vehicle to integrate and sustain what we've learned.

Here's an example that demonstrates what that meaning-making process could look like in action, one from the world of academia. Though Rick was an economics and finance major in college, math was never his strongest subject growing up. In high school, he always took the highest available course, but it was never much fun—and doing well took a lot of grinding. But in college, for the first time, math simply became a tool to better understand economic situations. When he recognized that, a light bulb went off: Math was simply a language, and he could use it to better understand and work with the

---

38 "Intentional Change Theory," Weatherhead School of Management.

world around him. Once he realized its potential, he re-contracted his relationship to math and began making an effort.

Suddenly, those courses came so much easier to him. Reframing math as a language was a complete game changer. The realization became a doorway to deeper learning—and more effective action.

In the integration phase, we must ask ourselves how we can drive a level of contextual learning that we can use across other domains of our existence.

In liminal space—and during the integration phase more specifically—the question becomes *How do we mindfully move past the initial learning to uncover a truly transformative moment, to learn something new about ourselves and/or the way the world works?*

That brings us to yet another question that is likely of significant benefit during this phase: *What is the greater level of integration that may come not only from the process but also from what I have just learned?* For Rick, the recognition that math is just a language became a gift that continues to give to this day, affecting his personal and professional approach and interactions. In the integration phase, we must ask ourselves how we can drive a level of contextual learning that we can use across other domains of our existence.

Similarly, during her equine leadership experience—which we discussed in chapter 6—Amy learned that her efforts to lead a horse through an obstacle course translated to her efforts to lead her team, to her parenting style, and to various other aspects of her life. Further, because she was outside her typical environment—a horse arena rather than her office or home—the learning occurred much more quickly than it would have in more familiar territory. Thus, the power of liminal space.

EMBRACING DECLARATIVE STATEMENTS

We've discussed the importance of understanding an experience, identifying what has been learned, and making meaning from it. But how do you truly drive that learning home? The next step is to make some declarations—to share those insights with someone else or with a group. Doing so deepens our understanding even more—as we not only learn to express the change we have observed and experienced but also open ourselves up to feedback from others. Making declarative statements allows us to reach another level in our evolution and makes our progress more likely to stick.

When making declarative statements to others, make sure to clearly communicate the *why* behind them. After all, if they don't know why this particular issue matters so much to you or your operation, they won't understand its urgency—or the purpose of their potential investment. (And remember, according to Boyatzis, that support is necessary to effectively institute change.) As communication expert Nancy Duarte explains, "If [your audience doesn't] know *why* a new action is necessary, they won't be motivated to help you."[39]

telos contends that you must also clarify *when* on the continuum you reside on your evolutionary journey. This is especially important when communicating with a team you hope will embrace the change you are talking about and take up the charge themselves. The ability to clearly identify that one has entered a period of discontinuity—a place of disproportionate opportunity—where transformational outcomes are truly possible can liberate a level of attention, discretionary effort,

---

39   Nancy Duarte, "Good Leadership Is About Communicating 'Why,'" Harvard Business Review, May 6, 2020, https://hbr.org/2020/05/good-leadership-is-about-communicating-why?utm_medium=email&utm_source=newsletter_daily&utm_campaign=dailyalert_activesubs&utm_content=signinnudge&referral=00563&deliveryName=DM79286.

and purposefulness equal to or even beyond a well-articulated *why*. Articulating both the *why* and the *when* ensures your declarative statements are positioned to make a lasting impact.

APPENDIX EXERCISE FOR THE INTEGRATION PHASE

- Impact Map

CHAPTER 10

sustainability.

Joseph Campbell developed the Hero's Journey, a twelve-stage pathway he built after studying myths and legends from numerous cultures and identifying a universal structure among them. While individual stories may avoid, repeat, or reorder various stages, most stages are present from tale to tale. For example, most stories begin by establishing the Ordinary World, in which we begin "to get to know the Hero and identify with him before the journey begins."[40] In this stage, he becomes a three-dimensional character with drives, urges, problems, and flaws.

The last stage is the Resurrection, in which the Hero is "reborn or transformed with the attributes of his Ordinary self in addition to the lessons and insights from the characters he has met along the road."[41] By the same token, to move from integration to sustainability in liminal space, one must metaphorically destroy one's former self to make space for the new self, with all of the attributes acquired along the way.

---

40 Christopher Vogler, foreword to *Myth and the Movies: Discovering the Mythic Structure of 50 Unforgettable Films* by Stuart Voytilla (Studio City, CA: Michael Wise Productions, 1999).

41 Vogler, foreword to *Myth and the Movies.*

Sustainability, the final stage of liminal space, is about truly embedding the learning and behavior changes identified and embodied in the previous phases into the operating system—whether individual or organizational. It is an ongoing commitment, one that requires discipline, evaluation, and recalibration to ensure we remain on track and that what we have chosen to integrate into our lives continues to serve us.

That doesn't mean sustainability requires constant effort. With the right tools and considerations, new approaches can become a way of thinking and being. For more insight into what sustainability looks like long term, we can turn to Mark Zeffiro. Mark had recently been named chief executive officer of Horizon Global when we began collaborating on a fitting venture for the CEO Award winners.

Mark called Rick one afternoon, shortly after the Horizon team returned from the Boulder Mail Trail. Rick was in a cab in New York, having flown there for some meetings. "What happened out there?" Mark asked. "These guys have literally transformed."

He reported that this group of engineers seemed to have found another gear within themselves. There was a thoughtfulness, an approachability, a team-based perspective that none of them had demonstrated previously. He went on to say, "The leadership venture platform has now become the primary mechanism for building and developing teams at Horizon Global Corporation."

A year later, Mark called us again. This time, it was personal. He and his son Trevor were at a pivotal point in their relationship. Trevor had just finished his undergraduate degree and was living back at home, but Mark felt as if they weren't aligned. He wanted to build a cohesiveness between them. He didn't want their relationship to get away from him. So, he decided that he and his son would participate in a telos Leadership Venture with Israel as the backdrop. Here, he shares how both experiences—sending his team on the venture and deciding to do one himself—have had an enduring impact on his perspective and approach.

When we decided to make the venture a part of our CEO Award, my team and I were in the process of integrating a business. The business produced engineered products that satisfied both local and global solutions, but we couldn't seem to agree on common default global goals. That presented a real challenge for us. How could we ask people to prioritize when we didn't have a common frame of reference?

We could always apply the typical financial or planning techniques, even under those circumstances, but there wasn't a sense of camaraderie or joint mission. We embarked on an effort to help our people understand each other first and foremost, and that began with this particular engagement.

The individuals we chose to participate in the Leadership Venture were very, very different. One was a fundamental introvert. Another was a man's man, for lack of a better phrase—someone comfortable in his own skin, who had been given great leadership opportunities throughout his career and tended to take control without prompting. And one was what I'd call a sideline watcher—different from the introvert. He clearly had a point of view, but he had never really stepped forward to express it before. Our objective was to take these three gentlemen from around the world, throw them in a pot, and see what happened.

We gave them a simple instruction: "When you come back, don't forget," we told them. We wanted to let them figure out how they would work together differently than they had in the past. That was the premise behind the entire effort.

What came of it? The introvert became an adept facilitator. The man's man became a mentor of sorts to the entire engineering process. The sideline watcher became a real leader, particularly when it came to identifying difficult technological solutions. Ultimately, we ended up with a team that could recommend priorities for the organization at large, adopting a perspective that wasn't limited to their engineering knowledge. Rather, each of them could contribute to the overall conversation on the business.

Right after the venture, they met the senior leadership team in Las Vegas to talk about their experience. I assumed that the man's man would lead the conversation, but he actually took a step back. The introvert ran the show.

We gave them a safe space to share, and it quickly became an emotional event. They were in tears, and so was the senior leadership team. They had torn down the artifice of their shells and been brought back to their bare nerves— the stuff that really motivates people. Fresh off the trail, they presented powerful ideas on how we could improve our creative process as a company—and also hold ourselves accountable to actually get things done.

That first Leadership Venture served as a fundamental pivot point for our integrated global programs. It resulted in our ability to share resources on a global scale. The leaders took it upon themselves to create their own engineering development program, in which other employees would spend time with each other in different places on the planet. To me, it was very clear that they had walked away with an understanding not only of themselves but also of how to play like a team—and how to help others do so too.

At this time, my son Trevor was facing some uncertainty. He had just finished school, and it was time for him to figure out what to do with his life. He had earned an applied mathematics degree in theoretical physics from Lehigh. He was generally interested in big data, but he couldn't quite articulate why or what or where or who or when. I could see the tension brewing beneath the surface.

We decided to participate in a Leadership Venture with the confluence of history, culture, and religious traditions in Israel as a formative catalyst.

I realized that I didn't have a true appreciation for the Leadership Venture experience until I did it myself. Until I saw what it did for my son.

On the venture, Rich suggested I give Trevor some space, so that he could have his own experience. With a little breathing room, he ultimately admitted that he was afraid. Afraid to admit what he really wanted to do. Afraid to fail. He was living with his mother and me in Detroit, and he didn't think he'd be able to find what he wanted to do there. He wanted to go to New York or California, but he feared he wouldn't have a place to come back to.

Sharing that served as a breakthrough for him. He realized that he didn't have to do it alone—that he could be willing to let others help him. He realized he could take a break from constantly doing something, take the earphones out of his ears, and take time to think in a quiet space that he had created for himself. And then he was able to take action.

Through the venture, I was also able to give him ownership over the events of his own life, to help him understand how he could deal with them for himself.

Growing up, I hadn't been given the same opportunity. I was raised in a very patriarchal family. I lost my grandfather—the closest friend I'd ever had—at age seven. My parents decided that I wouldn't get a chance to say goodbye. The choice was made for me.

Then, things got more complicated for my family. When I was twelve, my family went through a huge financial transformation. I was out of school for nearly a year, picking tobacco as a migrant worker. I carried the burden of those imposed experiences for decades, and finally, I had the chance to ask what they meant for my life. I could see that they had made me the guy who always goes in and helps other people fix things. But I had never learned how to do that for myself.

All of this rose to the surface on the venture, as I was transitioning out of my CEO role. At that point, I'd held aspiring roles with increasing levels of responsibility for more than thirty years. For me, this was an opportunity to take a half step back and ask why.

In Israel, as part of one of the exercises, we were tasked with picking a word that described what we were going through. I don't remember what Trevor's word was, but I do remember mine. I'd never been taken to my limit physically until that moment. The experience tore down all the defense mechanisms I had developed over time. My word became two words—a question, really: Why not?

Why not choose to do something different? Why not take that risk? Why not support my wife in developing her business?

My wife and I have been together for thirty years. We've traveled the world and lived on three different continents. My job has dragged me everywhere. I realized that this was my opportunity to look at the future differently, to think about my career challenge in a different way, to develop a new path forward—for both of us.

Since then, I've helped my wife buy some businesses that she actively runs, and I make sure everyone who works for her has what they need. I sit on a public company board. I've done some venture capital work. It's not necessarily what I thought I'd be doing at this stage of my life, but I'm happy.

Along the way, I've also found a new word: joy. Our society is often focused on the negative. As CEO of a company, you're always focused on forming the right message, rallying people in the right direction. So many of us have forgotten that joy is a choice—it's a choice you make each and every day when you get out of bed. It's something you can create. This curated liminal experience opened my eyes to a lot of things, many of which were already there— the potential for joy included.

My son experienced a significant transformation too. Today, he works for a startup big-data firm in Detroit—a role he found when he stopped focusing on the limitations of his circumstances and started seeing their potential. And he recently won a global award for an algorithm he built, beating out three thousand other companies. That reinforced for him that he could do great work and that he could do it anywhere. His brain is just as powerful in Detroit as it could be in New York or California.

Right now, he lives at home, not for lack of options, but because he has actually chosen to be here. In the meantime, he's stockpiling money. He bought himself a car outright with cash. He's building a nest egg to buy a condo. And we have a stronger relationship than we've ever had.

I've held on to what I learned in Israel. On the venture, we spent an hour of every day in complete silence. I still do it today, every day. It's my way of being spiritual. It allows my brain to slow down and focus on what matters. I also keep a page from a booklet telos gave me. It has reminders about how I want to live on it. I laminated it, and I keep it in my wallet, pulling it out whenever I need a refresher.

Today, I know I'm a better human than I was before. I'm a better father—by a football field—than I was when I was at the top of the professional ladder. To get there, I had to be willing to admit to myself that I wanted to go on a bit of a different journey and then commit to taking it day by day.

And I still remind myself that every day, every interaction is a chance to be joyful.

Intent versus Impact

Mark's story highlights the attention and commitment necessary to sustain real change in our lives. Just as the concept of re-contacting bridges catalyst and integration, evaluating intent versus impact is necessary to transition from integration to sustainability. Most of us know all too well that outcomes and results matter far more than intent. By the same token, while we may set out on our path to make change with clear and specific goals in mind, it is crucial to determine whether we are actually accomplishing what we aim to do.

Carve out space to reflect on your progress three, six, nine, and twelve months down the road. At each point, ask yourself whether the changes you have instituted have stuck—and whether they actually align with the intended impact you hoped to achieve. If not, it may be time to recalibrate. Formal tools like a 360-degree assessment can be helpful in this process. You'll also find an "Intent vs. Impact" exercise in the appendix.

Has Your Behavior Become Habit?

In 1926, Will Durant, an American writer, historian, and philosopher, summed up many of Aristotle's thoughts on morality in one clear, concise, and elegant sentence—one that is often attributed to Aristotle himself: "We are what we repeatedly do." That same sentiment becomes the marker for sustainability.

In determining whether we have transitioned from integration to sustainability, repetition comes into play. We must ask ourselves if we have operationalized what we've decided to do. Have we baked our decisions into our operating models? Do our outcomes reflect that? Have our desired behaviors become habit? In essence, have we created a behavior pattern such that breaking it would be more difficult than continuing to do it?

We must ask ourselves if we have operationalized what we've decided to do.

How do we know? Dr. Christine Whelan is a sociologist and clinical professor at the University of Wisconsin-Madison. She studies happiness, human ecology, and habits. She noted that behavior change is difficult, precisely because humans are creatures of habit. Whelan explained, "To make a change in our behavior, means we're adding something, or subtracting something, we have to figure out what it is. If I said, 'I want to go to the gym for an hour three times a week,' the first thing I'd have to figure out is, what am I *not* going to be doing during those hours ... So one great secret to succeeding at change is to be aware of what isn't going to happen once you start going to the gym."[42] As you embark

---

42   Brigid Schulte, "How to Build Good Habits—and Actually Make
      Them Stick," The Washington Post, March 2, 2015, https://
      www.washingtonpost.com/news/inspired-life/wp/2015/03/02/
      expert-ten-super-smart-ways-to-build-good-habits-and-make-them-stick/.

on the path toward sustainability, ask yourself which behaviors you'll be replacing with your new commitments and what it will take to make the switch.

It's also important not to attempt too many changes at once. Whelan said, "You basically do one at a time. If you're going to go to the gym, that's the one thing you're going to do. This year, I've been trying to reach out to more friends. That means I'm going to have to do a little less paid work or get less sleep. And I have to acknowledge that getting less sleep is a losing proposition for me, so I have to ask, 'Are my friends worth more than an hour of paid work?' If the answer is yes, then that's the choice I'm willing to make. That's it. That's the one thing I'm trying to change right now."[43]

If these potential behavior changes or habits seem specific, it's because specificity is key to effective change. You may be familiar with SMART goals, however, we've found that CLEAR goals, as developed by entrepreneur Adam Kreek, are more applicable to today's rapidly evolving and agile business environment.[44] CLEAR goals are

- collaborative, encouraging employees to work together;

- limited in both scope and duration;

- emotional, enabling employees to connect to them and tap into their own energy and passion;

- appreciable, broken down into smaller, more accomplishable goals that allow for long-term success; and

- refinable, clearly stated, but with room for modification as the situation or information develops [45]

43 Schulte, "How to Build Good Habits."

44 Peter Economy, "Forget SMART Goals—Try CLEAR Goals Instead," Inc., January 3, 2015, https://www.inc.com/peter-economy/forget-smart-goals-try-clear-goals-instead.html.

45 Economy, "Forget SMART Goals."

These elements allow for the establishment of goals "that can be built out, embraced, and acted upon by every member of the team."[46]

ADDRESSING UNPRODUCTIVE HABITS

Charles Duhigg, Pulitzer Prize–winning journalist and author of *The Power of Habit: Why We Do What We Do in Life and Business*, writes about how to investigate and break the less productive habits we have.

In his book, he shares a personal habit that he just couldn't kick: each afternoon at work, he would head to the cafeteria for a chocolate chip cookie. As a result, he had gained eight pounds—an outcome he wasn't very happy with.

He explains that the first step in breaking his habit was to understand how habits work. Each habit functions in the same three-part process. There is a cue, a routine, and a reward. First, a cue, or trigger, is established, launching the routine automatically, and that routine produces a reward—something that feels good, thus reinforcing the habit.

Duhigg began tracking his habit to determine the cue. He noticed that his cookie craving hit every day at around three o'clock in the afternoon. When that craving struck, he got up, headed to the cafeteria, bought his cookie, and ate it while talking to his coworkers before returning to his desk.

Duhigg knew that it is the reward—the last piece of the sequence that reinforces any habit. So, he had to find out what it was in his case. One day, he went outside and took a walk instead of getting a cookie. The next day, he got a candy bar rather than a cookie, and ate it at his desk. The day after that, he went to the cafeteria and didn't buy anything at all. Rather, he spent some time just talking with his

---

colleagues before he went back downstairs. That experimentation gave him insight into the reward he was actually after. He found that it wasn't the cookie; it was the social interaction.

Now, at three in the afternoon, instead of going to the cafeteria, he finds a friend to chat with for a bit. That chat has become his habit, taking the place of his cookie trek, and as a result, he has shed the weight. By diagnosing his habit, he could shift it. According to Duhigg, you can do the same.[47]

TO CHANGE YOUR HABITS, CHANGE YOUR ENVIRONMENT

There are other systemic factors to consider in the ongoing promotion of new behaviors and habits. We often say that we can't send a changed person into an unchanged system and expect that change to stick. Their surroundings must support their new approach. Research has demonstrated that to be true.

Wendy Wood, Provost Professor of Psychology and Business at the University of Southern California, conducts research on habits and why they are so challenging to break—including the role of environmental cues and their impact on habits and behavior. In one study, she found that those in the habit of making purchases at fast food restaurants continue to do so, even when they intended to stop. She stated, "Many of our repeated behaviors are cued by everyday environments, even though people think they're making choices all the time."[48] Thus, when we are attempting to develop habits we actually

---

47   Charles Duhigg, "How to Break Habits," YouTube video, 3:38. September 25, 2015, https://www.citationmachine.net/resources/cite-youtube-video/#:~:text=youtu. be%2FbO7FQsCcbD8-,Use%20the%20following%20structure%20to%20cite%20a%20 YouTube%20video%20in,Date%20published.

48   "Key to Changing Habits Is in Environment, Not Willpower, Duke Expert Says," Duke Today, December 13, 2007, https://today.duke.edu/2007/12/habit.html.

want to sustain, we must ask ourselves whether we have adjusted our environment to facilitate and maintain our behaviors.

Once we have re-contracted, determining that we want a new behavior to become a part of our lives, and begun integrating it into our thoughts and actions on a daily basis, we must consider the other inputs that would either enable or prevent it from continuing. For example, if you were committed to integrating something as simple as a daily exercise routine into your life, the next step would be to consider the factors that support or hinder the likelihood of sustaining. Perhaps you don't have a gym nearby and the track at the local high school is closed for renovations, both of which make it difficult to honor your commitment to working out. At that point, it's up to you to shape your environment to foster success, whether that means investing in some exercise equipment, downloading a fitness app, or finding a friend to run with multiple times a week. Including a friend, loved one, or colleague—an accountability partner of sorts—is a smart move, as it can have a powerful effect on sustainability as well.

> **We can't send a changed person into an unchanged system and expect that change to stick.**

At telos, we often hear about the impact of the social-support component of Leadership Ventures long after they come to an end. Participants feel a real sense of shared experience, and that fuels their interest in maintaining connections in the weeks, months, and years that follow. Those connections help them preserve not only the feel-good portion of their experience but also the accountability piece—the challenge of reshaping their work and lives to create a better existence for themselves and their communities. Why are these groups so effective at helping each other maintain accountability even after they return home? They spent time sharing their past experiences and completing difficult tasks with each other and received warm, authentic support in return.

For example, the Horizon team shifted their environment to support their individual goals by creating an ongoing communication rhythm—a social component to their personal growth. As such, even though they worked in different offices around the world, when they returned to their respective corners of the globe—where they were somewhat isolated from their experience on the trail—their interactions with each other helped them keep their learning and changed behaviors alike.

What if you're trying to formalize the culture and perspective of an entire organization? The structures of your operation must shift to consistently support the new approach. If, say, innovation is your goal, but senior leaders in your company tend to maintain the status quo or criticize others for speaking out of turn, your meeting culture, your approach, and even the stakeholders who are in attendance must change. For example, if you're hoping to cultivate innovation and still promoting based on tenure, the system must be altered to consistently recognize employees based primarily on potential.

Choice Is Inherent in Sustainability— and Every Phase of Liminality

We frequently ask our clients, *Is integration a feeling or a choice?* Ultimately, maintaining the behavior changes you have identified in the integration phase is a matter of choice. Each time you engage in those actions, you are deciding to honor your commitments—even when they begin to feel like habits. Changing behavior is hard work; it's easy to revert to former behaviors.

Meanwhile, if you wait for the "feeling" to move you to change, you'll probably find yourself stuck in your current ways. You have to make the choice every day to engage with the progress you'd like to make.

You've almost definitely experienced the role of choice even in your most conditioned behaviors. About a year ago, we moved a treadmill into our garage. For the past ten months, Amy has been out on that treadmill five—if not six—days a week. Still, there are days when she has to get up and make the decision to lace up her sneakers. Why? She knows if she doesn't do it for just a beat too long, that habit will be gone. When Rick ran the twenty-four-hour footrace we described in chapter 1, he found himself grappling with a similar decision: sustaining or advancing his pace required him to accept his current reality, including the discomfort it entailed, over and over again. The choice is ongoing, but it is always present. And to truly reach sustainability, we have to accept that.

In addition, we must also accept that in instituting our new set of behaviors and habits, we won't always be perfect. It can be challenging to remember that we have the choice to soldier on when we break our pattern, rather than giving up entirely—that it doesn't mean the game is over. Some weeks, Amy hits the treadmill only four days, rather than five or six. When that happens, she knows she must simply get back on track the next week. Just as Mark built in daily reminders to choose joy and honor the decisions he made in Israel, we need to take the time to remind ourselves why we chose to make a change in the first place.

In fact, we can think of those moments as catalysts in and of themselves: an opportunity to check in and reevaluate what we're doing, where we're headed, and whether we're on the right path. The choice to engage in that line of thinking is required to enter into liminal space again, to integrate any new information or understanding into our lives, and so on. In so many ways, it's the gift that keeps on giving.

APPENDIX EXERCISES FOR THE SUSTAINABILITY PHASE

- Balance Wheel
- My Gift
- 24-Hour Diary
- Intent v. Impact

what will you do? who will you be?

Many years ago, during a period of disruption in his personal and professional life, Rick entered a phase of great reflection and introspection. He methodically unpacked and assessed each aspect of his life—physical, mental, emotional, spiritual, and financial, among others.

As he continued to process the life he had built and the one he thought he wanted, a sense of fear began to emerge. What if he were to pursue the life he desired—with his priorities in the proper order and his values leading the way—only to discover that he wasn't smart enough, strong enough, or committed enough to make it happen?

He found himself marinating in his self-doubt, unable to move forward day after day. Then, a moment came when he sat at his desk, feeling particularly stagnant. He closed his eyes and imagined himself as an old man, reflecting on a life well lived. But the one that flashed before his eyes wasn't the path he envisioned—the aligned and well-prioritized future he had spent so long ruminating on. Instead, the future he pictured stemmed from where he sat right then, the place where he felt so stuck.

How would it feel to realize all those years later that he could have had the life he imagined, that it was all possible, had he simply taken the steps to manifest it?

Right then, his fear of discovering he couldn't was transformed into a far greater one: that he could have and simply never took the steps to find out. What a tragedy it would be to realize he could have created the life he wanted if only he hadn't allowed fear to impede his progress!

Now he lives every day willing to find out he can't do something, in service of what's possible. As you reflect on the liminal moments in your life, you will likely find yourself navigating a similar set of choices. It is our hope that you will use the tools you've found here to lean into the possibilities.

With the background you have built over the course of this book, you'll find that you are equipped to predict and harness opportunities for growth and change in your personal life, throughout your organization, and even in society at large—whether you find yourself in the midst of an in-between period unexpectedly or decide to launch one yourself.

With awareness and practice, we can get better at identifying, preparing for, and leveraging the inflection points in our lives.

In these pages, we've talked about identifying past liminal experiences—primarily those that have been imposed on us—and the provocative notion that, with what we have learned about those imposed periods, we can choose to trigger liminality ourselves. We've catalogued and dissected individual, team, and organizational examples of imposed and curated liminality alike, explored the four phases of liminal space, and provided tools to unlock the power of each one. Ultimately, this works to increase what we'll call liminal fitness: the concept that, with awareness and practice, we can get better at identifying, preparing for, and leveraging the inflection points in our lives.

To further illustrate the immense potential in effectively targeting and harnessing these moments, we can look to what we believe to be a societal inflection point. On May 25, 2020, police in Minneapolis, Minnesota, killed George Floyd, a black man, in the process of arresting him for allegedly using a counterfeit $20 bill. His death catalyzed protests around the country and across the world and brought tremendous attention to the Black Lives Matter movement. As of this writing, we are watching society work to reconcile its fraught history and recalibrate its current policies—from the legal system to the corporate ladder—in real time.

Similarly, as we write this in mid-2020, the novel coronavirus is reshaping healthcare around the globe. As more people express the desire and need to access practitioners without the risk of exposure, patients and practitioners alike are turning to tele-health—an option once limited by a host of regulations—and finding that the red tape that served as a deterrent for so many has all but disappeared. In addition, physicians and researchers are communicating across multiple channels and borders in hopes of finding new treatments and developing an effective vaccine, breaking down barriers previously enforced by bureaucracy and regulations.

These are just a couple of the tectonic shifts that we will continue to face in the coming weeks, months, and years. Climate change and limited water resources pose a dire threat to the health and well-being of people and our planet—and truly addressing them will require swift and sweeping action on the part of governments and individuals. Innovations in energy, synthetic biology, and computation have the potential to revolutionize society as we know it, ushering us into a new era—the likes of which we've never seen before—with its own unique challenges and opportunities.[49]

As such, we find ourselves in a period ripe for disruption in multiple arenas, where small shifts garner significant results. For example, nine months prior, someone attempting to advance social justice or healthcare technology by exerting 5 percent more energy toward the cause may have realistically expected a half percent return on that effort. Today, an investment of 5 percent more energy may result in a 50 percent return. The same logic and math apply to liminal periods of any size—including those that are personal, team-based, and organizational—demonstrating the business case for harnessing these opportunities.

With that in mind, you can see that the concept of liminal fitness comes into play: the ability to recognize and participate in the current momentum can have an extraordinary impact on what we can achieve. And building that liminal fitness—the capacity to weather tremendous change—may actually begin with a pause, of all things.

Is It Time for a Time-Out?

You'll remember the think weeks we discussed in chapter 6—time we set aside to leave behind the day-to-day and consider the past, present, and future of our business. Whether you are currently in the midst of a period of great uncertainty or hope to trigger or prepare for those to come, you may want to start with a similar practice—a time-out to reflect on where you are and where you want to go.

---

49   Gregg Satell, "These Three Technology Inflection Points Will Change Our Future Beyond Recognition," Inc., January 27, 2019, https://www.inc.com/greg-satell/these-3-technology-inflection-points-will-change-our-future-beyond-recognition.html.

It's not just our personal experience that points to the validity of such an endeavor—research supports the power of taking a pause. Ruth Wageman is a professor at Harvard University and one of the world's foremost scholars on teams and team performance. She found that, when it comes to quantifying team effectiveness, 60 percent depends on design, which encompasses the types of members that compose the group, its overarching purpose, and its collaborative style. Moreover, she found that a team's launch determines 30 percent of its performance, another element that should be accounted for in the design process.[50] Despite its importance, many teams lack the kind of clarity of design necessary for success—particularly when leaders and managers are attempting to navigate uncharted territory, such as the business implications of a global pandemic.

Taking time to think through your organization's dynamics—and if a relaunch may be necessary—can help you harness opportunities as they present themselves. But before you make any moves, make sure you are checking in with yourself.

Author and leadership expert Margaret Wheatley suggests creating "islands of sanity" for leaders—particularly in turbulent times—to allow for greater visibility and clarity. She writes,

"It is possible, in this time of profound disruption, for leadership to be a noble profession that contributes to the common good. It is possible, as we face the fearful complexity of life-destroying problems, to experience recurring moments of grace and joy. It is possible, as leaders of organizations, communities, and families, to discover deep and abiding satisfaction in our work if we choose not to flee or withdraw from reality. It is possible to find a path of contribution and meaning if we turn our attention away from issues beyond our

---

50   Ruth Wageman and Krister Lowe, "Designing, Launching, and Coaching Teams" in *The Practitioner's Handbook of Team Coaching*, ed. David Clutterbuck et al. (New York: Routledge, 2019).

control and focus on the people around us who are yearning for good leadership and engage them in work that is within reach. It is possible to use our influence and power to create *islands of sanity* in the midst of a raging destructive sea."[51]

She continues, "So much is possible if we consciously and wisely choose how best to step forward as leaders for this time."[52] To proceed consciously and wisely, we must take the time to absorb the chaos of the world around us and prepare for what will come next, determining not only what we will do but also who we will choose to be.

What Do You Stand for—and What Are You Willing to Change?

How do you ensure you're ready for moments like these? It begins with self-awareness—getting in touch with your values and committing to live them, for the benefit of yourself, your team, and your organization. Do you know your strengths—what you already do well—as well as the areas in which you need help? Are you clear on your purpose, and how it affects your everyday life? What is enduring for you, and what are you ready and willing to change? Review the "My Gift" exercise in the appendix to uncover your unique contributions.

Locating your values can help you find direction and meaning, even in the midst of overwhelming uncertainty, as one of our clients realized recently. As COVID continued to spread throughout the country and across the world, we moved all our engagements online, including our annual Renewal and Discovery professional development experience.

---

51   Margaret Wheatley, *Who Do We Choose to Be? Facing Reality Claiming Leadership Restoring Sanity* (Oakland, CA: Berrett-Koehler, 2017).

52   Wheatley, *Who Do We Choose to Be?*

One day, Rick was on a video coaching call with a woman who had been participating in the experience, which included small cohorts that convened on a regular basis to provide each other with connection and support. During the call, they were discussing a values exercise that had been facilitated in her cohort.

"I realized that my organization's values don't align with mine," she said, scanning her notes to share more about what she had discovered. As her thoughts began to crystalize, she blurted out, "My organization doesn't value 'love.'"

Then she looked straight into the camera and said, "But yours does."

In the midst of that unprecedented time, telos remained committed to proceeding with love—and that commitment made our work all the more possible and all the more gratifying. Moreover, it was having an impact outside our organization as well.

When you know what you stand for, you will be better prepared to take advantage of the circumstances that present for the benefit of your conscience, your culture, and your bottom line—in a manner that aligns with your beliefs. Considering these questions also enhances your and your organization's ability to think at scale—understanding how your values and beliefs persist as your operation grows. Ultimately, it comes down to choice. To fully harvest the power of liminal space, you must choose to mindfully engage with it. As the Greek stoic philosopher Epictetus wrote, though life might be subject to constant change, human beings are ultimately responsible for how they interpret and respond to those changes. To build further clarity on your foundation, you may want to return to our discussion on the preparation phase in chapter 7.

With a framework for readiness, you may be wondering what happens next.

Where Do I Go from Here?

If you're still reading, you see the value in navigating these periods of inflection. You've come to understand the importance of meeting uncertainty with preparation, practice, and a set of principles that serve as a guiding force, even as you enter the choppiest of waters. Now, you have the knowledge to dig into past liminal experiences for greater insight. And you've developed an awareness of how you might use that information to curate liminality for yourself, your team, and your organization. You are ready to approach the various realms in which you reside through a new lens, widening the aperture to let in more light in the form of information, questions, and uncertainty. But you don't have to do it alone.

Over the years, we've seen the power of this process play out for so many others. We've had the privilege of serving as a trusted advisor and partner to individuals and operations of all sizes as they reimagine their business strategies, make their way through liminal space, and institute sustainable improvements to their structure and processes. If you're looking for help navigating the challenges and opportunities in front of you—and accelerating in the direction of success—we are here to help.

And regardless of the path you choose to take, we wish you the strength, courage, and insight to unleash the power of liminal space— and thereby liberate the greatness within you and all those around you.

about the authors.

Rick Simmons and Amy Simmons founded the telos institute in 2006 to offer specialized expertise in business strategy, leadership development, and change management to leaders, leadership teams, and organizations around the world.

Rick serves as a trusted advisor and coach to the world's foremost leaders, leadership teams, and organizations. As CEO, he is responsible for the firm's vision and strategy, while inspiring a growing cohort of world-class practitioners to deliver transformational experiences for clients.

Previously, he served in various senior strategy and sales leadership positions within the financial services industry. Most notably, he led several organizations through periods of transition, which has afforded him unique insight into change management best practices.

An accomplished organizational development professional, Amy has spent over two decades collaborating across numerous levels of leadership and industries to help individuals, teams, and companies thrive. Her extensive experience in coaching, workshop design and implementation, and large- and small-group facilitation inform her unique ability to identify and support client development needs as Chief Experience Officer.

Prior to founding telos, Amy held coaching, training, career management, and recruiting roles and conducted extensive research on adult learning theory and curriculum and course development.

Both Rick and Amy hold master of science degrees in organization development and analysis from the Weatherhead School of Management at Case Western Reserve University.

exercises.

personal balance wheel

Within each of the following eight areas, circle the number that best represents your level of satisfaction in that area of your life.

(7 = completely satisfied; 1 = completely dissatisfied)

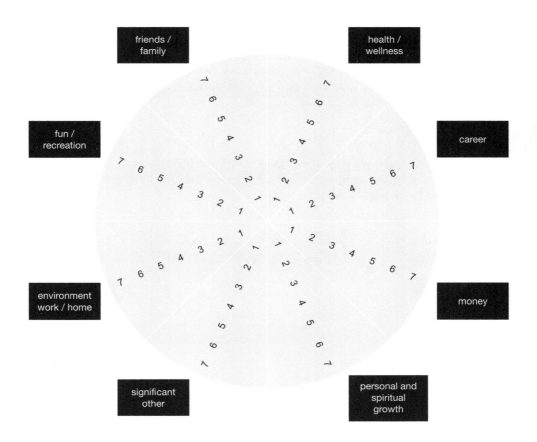

Each of us embodies a unique combination of skills, experiences, personality, intellect, and ambition. In essence, the uniqueness and rarity of this combination is an asset to the world around us. As you reflect on yourself in this way, consider how this uniqueness manifests itself each day.

phase I

Review any / all leadership assessments you've taken in the past; considered together, what patterns emerge?

> › Ask yourself. "In what direction am I focusing this rare combination of attributes?"

phase II

Now, take your exploration a step outward. Ask family, friends, colleagues – those who are important to you – what they perceive to be your gift(s). Seek to learn what they most appreciate about you; in what circumstances they look to you; and what defines the unique set of gifts you bring to the world.

phase III

Consider all the data you've gathered to date – through assessment review, feedback, exercises, journaling, etc. – and begin to clarify the gift you want to give the world.

> › How does your gift currently manifest itself?
>
> › What additional opportunities exist for you to give your gift?
>
> › What gets in the way of you giving your gift?

1. Determine your core values.

From the list below, highlight every core value that resonates with you. Do not overthink your selection. As you read through the list, select the words that feel like a core value to you personally. If you think of a value you possess that is not on the list, write it down.

Abundance	Collaboration	Flexibility	Originality	Perfection
Acceptance	Consistency	Happiness	Passion	Playfulness
Accountability	Contribution	Health	Performance	Popularity
Achievement	Creativity	Honesty	Personal Development	Power
Adventure	Credibility	Humility	Proactive	Preparedness Security
Advocacy	Curiosity	Humor	Professionalism	Self-Control
Ambition	Daring Decisiveness	Inclusiveness	Proactivity	Selflessness
Appreciation	Dedication	Independence	Professionalism	Simplicity
Attractiveness	Dependability	Individuality	Punctuality	Stability
Autonomy	Diversity	Innovation	Quality	Success Teamwork
Balance	Empathy	Inspiration	Recognition	Thankfulness
Being the Best	Encouragement	Intelligence	Relationships	Thoughtfulness
Benevolence	Enthusiasm	Intuition Joy	Reliability	Traditionalism
Boldness	Ethics	Kindness	Resilience	Trustworthiness
Brilliance	Excellence	Knowledge	Resourcefulness	Understanding
Calmness	Expressiveness	Leadership	Responsibility	Uniqueness
Caring	Fairness	Learning	Responsiveness	Usefulness
Challenge	Family	Love	Risk Taking	Versatility
Charity	Friendships	Loyalty	Safety	Vision
Cheerfulness	Flexibility	Making a Difference	Security	Warmth
Cleverness	Freedom	Mindfulness	Service	Wealth
Community	Fun	Motivation	Spirituality	Well-Being
Commitment	Generosity	Optimism	Stability	Wisdom
Compassion	Grace	Open-Mindedness	Peace	Zeal
Cooperation	Growth			

2. Group all similar values together from the list of values you just created.

Group them in a way that makes sense to you personally. Create a maximum of five groupings. If you have more than five groupings, drop the least important grouping(s).

example

Abundance	Acceptance	Appreciation	Balance	Cheerfulness
Growth	Compassion	Encouragement	Health	Fun
Wealth	Inclusiveness	Thankfulness	Personal Development	Happiness
Security	Intuition	Thoughtfulness	Spirituality	Humor
Freedom	Kindness	Mindfulness	Well-being	Inspiration
Independence	Love			Joy
Flexibility	Making a Difference			Optimism
Peace	Open-Mindedness			Playfulness
	Trustworthiness			
	Relationships			

my values

186

3. Choose one word within each grouping that represents the label for the entire group.

Again, do not overthink your labels – there are no right or wrong answers. You are defining the answer that is right for you. See the example below – the label chosen for the grouping is bolded. Highlight your selection in the grid on page 2.

example

Abundance	Acceptance	Balance Health	Cheerfulness
Growth Wealth	Compassion	Personal Development	Fun
Security **Freedom**	Inclusiveness	Spirituality	**Happiness**
Independence	Intuition	**Well-being**	Humor
Flexibility	Kindness Love		Inspiration Joy
	Making a Difference		Optimism
Peace	Open-Mindedness		Playfulness
	Trustworthiness		
	Relationships		

Appreciation	
Encouragement	
Thankfulness	
Thoughtfulness	
Mindfulness	

4. Add a verb to each value (so you can see what it looks like as an actionable core value, for example):

^ Live in freedom
^ Seek opportunities for making a difference
^ Act with mindfulness
^ Promote well-being
^ Multiply happiness

This will guide you in the actions you need to take to feel like you are truly living on purpose.

my values ↑ ↑ ↑ ↑

5. Finally, capture your core values in order of priority in a visible, easily accessible place

(i.e. your phone, card on your desk, etc.), so they are available as an easy reference when you are faced with decisions. For example:

1) Live in freedom
2) Act with mindfulness
3) Promote well-being
4) Multiply happiness
5) Seek opportunities for making a difference

my values

Please complete the following exercise with someone close to you (spouse, trusted friend, etc.):

Imagine it's 7 years from today and your life has grown into more than you ever hoped or dreamed. Each facet of your life has evolved well beyond any pragmatic or expected outcome. As you consider life through this fantastic lens of the future, consider the following questions, and please, resist the urge to be reasonable or practical. Giving yourself license to dream can help unearth the elements you deem necessary for creating a robust and vibrant future in the real world. Also, as you consider this lottery-winning view of life, challenge yourself to be as specific as possible, even strive to imagine how your life would unfold over a specific 24-hour period of time.

> When do you wake up?
> Who do you live and socialize with?
> Who do you see and talk to?
> Which relationships are most important?
> What do you think about most?
> What occupies the largest part of your day?
> What are your most valued possessions?
> What has been your crowning achievement?
> What is the next goal that you're pursuing?
> What do you do for fun?
> Are you working? If yes, describe your work.
> What are your major responsibilities?
> Where are you?
> Where do you spend your time?
> How do you spend your free time?
> How do you feel?

Consider the re-interpreted belief that has emerged for you during curated liminality.

Will this impact those around you? How? Will it be beneficial to share this new way of being with any / all of the groups below? Start by capturing your insights on the top of page two. Next, identify specific people within each wedge of the circle. Finally, plan how / if you will share these insights with each individual / group.

insights from curated liminality

belief	behavior	insights	re-interpreted belief	new behavior
i.e. I am too direct with most people.	i.e. I avoid sharing my opinions.	i.e. My directness is my gift.	i.e. I can be soft on the person and direct in sharing my thoughts.	i.e. I directly share my thoughts / opinions when appropriate while showing care for the person.

COMMUNICATION PLAN

WHO…	WILL I COMMUNICATE MY NEW INSIGHTS? HOW?
supervisor	
individual direct reports	

WILL I COMMUNICATE MY NEW INSIGHTS? HOW?

WHO...

team (as a whole)

peers

organization

family / friends / community

Keep a log of your activities for at least two different 24-hour periods of time.

Be thoughtful and feel free to vary the types of days when you capture data: i.e. weekday vs. weekend day or workday vs. non-work day. The goal is not to make judgments about how you utilize your time; instead, to simply raise your awareness to how you're currently using this precious resource and help you better align the use of your time with what is most important.

Be sure to make your entries as the day progresses; do not wait until the end of the 24-hour period to populate your diary. Tracking as you go will alter your activities a little, but that's okay. Decide on your own how often you will make an entry; please do not wait more than 3 hours before making your notes though.

Make your entries as complete as you can, and fill in the details of the events that were significant to you.

Improving our interactions with others is often rooted in
1) better articulating our internally known intentions, and
2) effectively aligning our outwardly experienced impact.
Use the following questions and rhythm of self check-ins
to better calibrate your behaviors and elevate your intentions.

intent

With what area of your life
are you re-contracting?

impact (3 months)

In your development area,
identify an instance when
you recently and clearly
expressed your intention.

How did you perceive the
impact of your intention?

How did others perceive
the impact of your
intention?

What subsequent and
specific behaviors aligned
with your intention?

Was this impact in
alignment with your
intention?

What, if any, recalibration
is needed for greater
alignment of intent and
impact?

impact (6 months)

In your development area, identify an instance when you recently and clearly expressed your intention.

How did you perceive the impact of your intention?

How did others perceive the impact of your intention?

What subsequent and specific behaviors aligned with your intention?

Was this impact in alignment with your intention?

What, if any, recalibration is needed for greater alignment of intent and impact?

impact (12 months)

In your development area, identify an instance when you recently and clearly expressed your intention.

How did you perceive the impact of your intention?

How did others perceive the impact of your intention?

What subsequent and specific behaviors aligned with your intention?

Was this impact in alignment with your intention?

What, if any, recalibration is needed for greater alignment of intent and impact?